# Su...

# LO...
# SIGNS

GW01451332

# TAURUS
## 20 APRIL—20 MAY

### by Jacqui Deevoy

Your heavenly guide to
LIFE, LOVE and BOYS

It's cosmic!

mustard

First published in 1999 by Mustard

Mustard is an imprint of Parragon

Parragon
Queen Street House
4 Queen Street
Bath BA1 1HE
UK

Produced by Magpie Books, an imprint of
Robinson Publishing Ltd, London

Text © Jacqui Deevoy 1999
Sugar Love Signs © 1999 Sugar Ltd. Licensed with TLC

All rights reserved. This book is sold subject to the condition
that it shall not, by way of trade or otherwise, be lent, re-sold,
hired out or otherwise circulated in any form of binding or cover
other than that in which it is published and without a similar
condition including this condition being imposed on the
subsequent purchaser.

Page design by Sandie Boccacci

ISBN 1-84164-192-8

A copy of the British Library Cataloguing-in-Publication Data is
available from the British Library

Printed and bound in the EC

# Contents

# Part 10: YOUR YEAR AHEAD: THE YEAR 2000 AT A GLANCE

# Part 11: INTO THE NEW MILLENNIUM!

# Part 12: BIRTHDAY CHART

# For all my favourite Taureans:

Martin
Cherée
Jayne
Georgina
Julian
Sandra
John
Jock
Lee
Caroline
Jane
Tuesday
Winnie
Mel
Aaron
Sandra
John

# Part 1:
# All About Taurus

# A Brief Introduction To Your Sign . . .

Taurus is the second sign of the zodiac and is concerned with beauty, sensuality, possessions, talents and wealth. Ruled by the planet Venus, you're affectionate, patient and trustworthy. It's Venus you also have to thank for your love of beauty and luxury. Your best qualities are your dependability, your kindness, your calm and your strength of character. But being a Taurus, the sign of the bull, there's another, not so positive, side to your personality . . . You're sometimes accused of being stubborn, inflexible, possessive and self-indulgent. And although you're kind, you're not always generous. (The Taurean motto could easily be: "What's yours is mine; and what's mine is mine too!"). You're a real slow mover, and often miss out on opportunities because you take so long wondering and pondering . . . But a lot of that's due to the fact that you hate being rushed – in fact, it can make you feel quite panicky if you have to do something within a certain time limit. You'd rather not do it all than do it feeling that way.

You were a very quiet, placid baby. You were probably shy and found occasions where you were the centre of attention – your own birthday parties, for example – a bit much to cope with. You were an affectionate little thing though and loved nothing more than a good old cuddle. Aw . . .

You like to know where you are and where you stand and, because of this, have a real dislike of change. You have a tendency to take everything and everyone at face value and, because your sense of judgment isn't that spot-on, this could hold you back. Concentrate on developing your intuition though and things will improve.

The overriding need of a Taurean is security – practically and emotionally. You like routine (it makes you feel safe), being in a romantic relationship, and some cash stashed away for a rainy day.

You can come across as a shy type who has little to say, but when you relax, what you do come out with is always interesting. Unlike some of the other more garrulous signs, you only really speak when you've got something worthwhile to say – otherwise, you'll just stay schtum.

**Here you are in a nutshell:**

**You're great . . .** because you're calm, attentive and very gentle.

**You grate . . .** because you do everything in your own sweet time (and that's an irritatingly long time to some people!), you've got a nasty temper and you can be incredibly pig-headed.

**You rate . . .** singing, having wads of cash and sleeping.

**You hate . . .** change, being rushed and sharing your possessions.

**You're late . . .** never! You're the most reliable sign of the zodiac. If you say you'll be somewhere at a certain time, you'll be there. That's just the sort of person you are.

**As a mate . . .** you're trustworthy, loyal but sometimes jealous.

**As a date . . .** you're faithful, sexy but unforgiving.

**Your fate:** To learn the meaning of insight.

# Lucky Stuff

**Numbers:** 2 (because you're the second sign of the zodiac); and 6 (the traditional number associated with Taurus and Venus, your ruling planet).

**Day:** Friday (the weekend starts here – hurrah!).

**Colour:** Pale pink (which shows your soft side) and all shades of blue and green (indicative of your honesty and love of the great outdoors).

**Gemstone:** Sapphire, emerald and topaz – gorgeously sparkling (just how you like to be seen!).

**Metal:** Copper (wear a copper bracelet for luck).

**Flowers:** Daisies, poppies and violets. Sweet and girly – just like you!

**Food:** Golden Grahams, Pop Tarts, fruit salad and a big spicy curry! (Not all on the same plate though . . .)

**Animal:** Bull.

**Bird:** Dove.

**Cities:** Hastings, Dublin, Lucerne and St Louis. If you're a Taurean living in one of these cities already, count yourself extra lucky!

# Your Rising Sign = The You Others See

*In astrology, if you want to discover more about your outer personality and how you come across to others, it helps if you know your Ascendant. Working it out can be a problem, but using the specially devised chart over the page, it couldn't be easier. So look yourself up . . .*

## A Bit About Rising Signs

Your Rising Sign is the main indicator of your outer personality (i.e. how others see you as opposed to how you view yourself) and also has a major bearing on the way you look and the impact you make on the opposite sex. When combined with your Sun Sign, you'll get an even more accurate picture.

It's important to take British Summer Time into account when working out your Rising Sign. This period varies from year to year but, to keep things simple, if you were born between March 16 and October 31 of any year, subtract one hour from your time of birth. If you were born between midnight and 1 a.m. during the Summer Time period, your birth hour will be 11 p.m. or 12 midnight on the previous day. If you're uncertain about your birth time, all you can do is read through all twelve descriptions on the following pages and see if you can spot yourself. It shouldn't be difficult.

Born abroad? Well, find out the time difference between the United Kingdom and your place of birth. If you were born in a country that is ahead of the UK time-wise, then subtract the number of hours' difference from your birth time; if you were born in a country that's behind the UK time-wise, then add that number of hours to your birth time.

## How To Use The Rising Signs Chart

**1.** Locate your birth date in the first (left-hand) column on the chart on pages 8 and 9.

**2.** Find your birth hour along the top of the page. If you were born between hours, work it out to the nearest hour. For example, if you were born at 8.45 a.m., your birth hour is 9 a.m. If you were born at 6.20 p.m., your birth hour is 6 p.m. If you were born at exactly half past the hour, go to the next hour (i.e. being born at 4.30 a.m. would give you the birth hour of 5 a.m.) Don't forget to subtract an hour if you were born between March 16 and October 31.

**3.** At the point where the two columns meet, you'll find an astrological symbol. Look up this symbol in the Symbol Index on page 10 and find out what your Rising Sign is.

**4.** Then turn the page, find your Rising Sign and discover more about the way others – blokes included! – perceive you. **Note:** If the description doesn't sound like you, check the sign before and after. Because the chart is general, 100 per cent accuracy is impossible for everyone who uses it, and some people may, by the skin of their teeth, fall into the wrong category.

# RISING SIGNS CHART

| TIME ▶<br><br>DATE ▼ | 1 AM | 2 AM | 3 AM | 4 AM | 5 AM | 6 AM | 7 AM | 8 AM | 9 AM | 10 AM |
|---|---|---|---|---|---|---|---|---|---|---|
| Jan 1–16 | ♎ | ♏ | ♏ | ♏ | ♐ | ♐ | ♑ | ♑ | ♒ | ♓ |
| Jan 17–Feb 21 | ♏ | ♏ | ♐ | ♐ | ♑ | ♑ | ♑ | ♒ | ♓ | ♈ |
| Feb 22–Mar 29 | ♐ | ♑ | ♑ | ♒ | ♒ | ♓ | ♈ | ♉ | ♉ | ♊ |
| Mar 30–Apr 29 | ♑ | ♒ | ♓ | ♓ | ♈ | ♉ | ♊ | ♊ | ♋ | ♋ |
| Apr 30–May 19 | ♒ | ♓ | ♈ | ♈ | ♉ | ♊ | ♊ | ♋ | ♋ | ♌ |
| May 20–Jun 8 | ♓ | ♈ | ♉ | ♊ | ♊ | ♋ | ♋ | ♌ | ♌ | ♌ |
| Jun 9–24 | ♈ | ♉ | ♊ | ♊ | ♋ | ♋ | ♋ | ♌ | ♌ | ♍ |
| Jun 25–Jul 17 | ♉ | ♊ | ♊ | ♋ | ♋ | ♌ | ♌ | ♌ | ♍ | ♍ |
| Jul 18–Aug 14 | ♊ | ♊ | ♋ | ♋ | ♌ | ♌ | ♍ | ♍ | ♍ | ♎ |
| Aug 15–Sep 19 | ♋ | ♋ | ♌ | ♌ | ♌ | ♍ | ♍ | ♎ | ♎ | ♎ |
| Sep 20–Oct 29 | ♌ | ♌ | ♍ | ♍ | ♎ | ♎ | ♎ | ♏ | ♏ | ♐ |
| Oct 30–Dec 8 | ♍ | ♍ | ♍ | ♎ | ♎ | ♏ | ♏ | ♏ | ♐ | ♐ |
| Dec 9–31 | ♎ | ♎ | ♏ | ♏ | ♐ | ♐ | ♐ | ♑ | ♑ | ♒ |

| 11 AM | 12 NOON | 1 PM | 2 PM | 3 PM | 4 PM | 5 PM | 6 PM | 7 PM | 8 PM | 9 PM | 10 PM | 11 PM | 12 M'NT |
|---|---|---|---|---|---|---|---|---|---|---|---|---|---|
| ♓ | ♈ | ♉ | ♊ | ♊ | ♋ | ♋ | ♌ | ♌ | ♌ | ♍ | ♍ | ♎ | ♎ |
| ♈ | ♉ | ♊ | ♊ | ♋ | ♋ | ♌ | ♌ | ♍ | ♍ | ♎ | ♎ | ♎ | ♏ |
| ♊ | ♋ | ♋ | ♌ | ♌ | ♍ | ♍ | ♍ | ♎ | ♎ | ♎ | ♏ | ♏ | ♐ |
| ♋ | ♌ | ♌ | ♍ | ♍ | ♍ | ♎ | ♎ | ♏ | ♏ | ♏ | ♐ | ♐ | ♑ |
| ♌ | ♌ | ♍ | ♍ | ♎ | ♎ | ♎ | ♏ | ♏ | ♐ | ♐ | ♐ | ♑ | ♑ |
| ♍ | ♍ | ♍ | ♎ | ♎ | ♏ | ♏ | ♏ | ♐ | ♐ | ♑ | ♑ | ♒ | ♓ |
| ♍ | ♍ | ♎ | ♎ | ♏ | ♏ | ♏ | ♐ | ♐ | ♑ | ♑ | ♒ | ♒ | ♓ |
| ♎ | ♎ | ♎ | ♏ | ♏ | ♐ | ♐ | ♐ | ♑ | ♑ | ♒ | ♓ | ♈ | ♉ |
| ♎ | ♎ | ♏ | ♏ | ♐ | ♐ | ♑ | ♑ | ♒ | ♒ | ♓ | ♈ | ♉ | ♉ |
| ♏ | ♏ | ♐ | ♐ | ♐ | ♑ | ♑ | ♒ | ♓ | ♈ | ♈ | ♉ | ♊ | ♊ |
| ♐ | ♐ | ♑ | ♑ | ♒ | ♓ | ♈ | ♉ | ♉ | ♊ | ♊ | ♋ | ♋ | ♌ |
| ♑ | ♑ | ♒ | ♓ | ♓ | ♈ | ♉ | ♊ | ♊ | ♋ | ♋ | ♋ | ♌ | ♌ |
| ♒ | ♓ | ♈ | ♉ | ♊ | ♊ | ♋ | ♋ | ♌ | ♌ | ♌ | ♍ | ♍ | ♎ |

## Symbol Index

ᙏ Aries
ᙎ Taurus
ᚋ Gemini
ᚏ Cancer
ᚐ Leo
ᙢ Virgo
ᙍ Libra
ᙣ Scorpio
ᙨ Sagittarius
ᙥ Capricorn
ᙤ Aquarius
ᙦ Pisces

**If your Rising Sign is ARIES (ᙏ)**, you're striking looking, with bold (though not necessarily even) features, a bony angular face and fine hair. Most females with Aries Rising are of average height, but because of their "big" personalities, they often come across as taller. Aries rules the head and this could be why you're so often described as headstrong. Others see you as dynamic, assertive and impulsive, and you tend to attract people who are just as lively as you. The Aries motto is "I am" and you can come across as rather self-centred. But it can also make you appear confident and focused – both very attractive qualities. Boys love you but are sometimes put off by your forcefulness. If they are, then they're the ones who are going to lose out . . .

**If your Rising Sign is TAURUS (♉)**, your personality is as strong and solid as your body. Females with Taurus Rising tend to be short to medium height, but make up for any lack of stature with amazing strength. You can recognize a Taurus Rising type by her square face and thick curly – usually dark – hair. Taurus rules the throat and neck and this may be why you have such a sexy and seductive voice. What people like most about you is the fact you're so down-to-earth and trustworthy – that's the way they see you anyway. The Taurus motto is "I have" and this way of thinking can cause you to be rather possessive. Unless you can curb this part of your personality – and it needs restraining because it shows itself almost as soon as you meet somebody – it could be off-putting, especially when you're trying to pull. When it comes to love, you can be a bit shy, but once you find a bloke who makes you feel secure and sexy, you'll relax and let it all hang out.

**If your Rising Sign is GEMINI (♊)**, you're fast in every way – light on your feet, quick-thinking and an incessant chatterer – and this gives an impression of you being younger than you are. Girls with Gemini Rising tend to be medium height and very slim. You may be a tad flat-chested but you're by no means boyish – you're all woman and proud of it! You've got a cheeky expression with sparkling eyes and long arms and legs (the parts of the body ruled by Gemini). You're always on the go and never seem to finish one project before starting another. You reckon this is due to your flea-like concentration span, but other people think it's down to the fact that you're multi-talented! The Gemini motto is "I talk" and while this can be attractive to some people, it can put others right off, especially when your mouth runs away with you. Boys find you irresistible – once you learn to talk less and listen more you're bound to find the guy of your dreams.

**If your Rising Sign is CANCER (♋)**, you have an intelligent face with twinkling eyes and a smiling mouth. Your hair is very fine and it's often either very blonde or very dark – invariably dyed. Cancer rules the bosom and you certainly have one large enough for all your mates to use as a pillow (metaphorically speaking of course!). When you first meet others, you come across as rather tough, even though underneath you're a right old softie. The Cancer motto is "I feel" and this is something which may surprise your mates. But you are, in fact, deeply sensitive and you're not doing yourself any favours by hiding this. See this quality as an asset, not a handicap, and you'll become instantly more attractive.

**If your Rising Sign is LEO (♌)**, you have thick, wavy hair, which you like to wear back off your face. You have a lovely smiley expression and this makes you very attractive to others. As a Leo Rising female, you may be short, but because you have good posture, your lack of stature usually goes unnoticed. Leo rules the heart and when it comes to others your heart is very big indeed. In fact, you strive to make people – especially boys – like you and would be well miffed if you discovered that someone – *anyone* – found you disagreeable. The Leo motto is "I create" and so it should be – because you're a very imaginative person. If your life ever gets boring, you'll do whatever you can to liven it up. And if you get totally tired of being you (which seems to happen from time to time), you're perfectly capable of using your creative powers to re-invent yourself. Which is fine as long as the real you doesn't get lost in the process.

**If your Rising Sign is VIRGO (♍)**, you're a lively, chatty person with an inquisitive nature and expression. You're probably tall and, although you may be slim, you're destined to fill out as you get older! However horizontally challenged you become though, you'll always have fab legs! You may feel a bit of a wimp sometimes, but Virgo rules the stomach; maybe that's why other people see you as having plenty of guts! If something displeases you, you're certainly not going to sit there in silence – oh no. If a complaint's being made, it's more than likely Miss Virgo Rising who's making it! The Virgo motto is "I serve", which sounds a bit sad, but just illustrates how willing you are to help others. In a romantic

relationship, you do run the risk of being taken for granted, so it's important that you make yourself clear at the very start. You're fussy about boyfriends, but in your view the fewer you date, the fewer you have to dump and the more fun you have.

**If your Rising Sign is LIBRA (♎)**, you're gorgeously female and attractive, with a shapely figure and a pretty face. You're average to tall in height and have beautiful hair. Libra rules the spine and no one who knows you would ever call you spineless. In fact, you have your own particular brand of courage and forthrightness, which occasionally translates as arrogance but is often charming. This doesn't wash with your female friends, but goes down a treat with the blokes, who seem to interpret it as a kind of sexual confidence. The Libra motto is "I consider", which *should* make you discerning but in actual fact means you'll basically consider anyone! You find it very hard to say "no" to boys and this can get you into tricky situations. And although you like an easy life, you don't mind a romantic complication every now and again.

**If your Rising Sign is SCORPIO (♏)**, you have an unusual face, with a well-defined jawline, a wide mouth and amazing eyes. Your figure is curvy (though not necessarily slim) and your hair is thick and naturally wavy. You're an inquisitive person by nature – this

may be heightened by the fact that the sign of Scorpio rules the nose! Other people see you as a real cool customer and a few may even be a bit scared of you. They know how clever and intuitive you are and because you give the impression that you're hard, they may regard you as a force to be reckoned with. Which, of course, you are . . . The Scorpio motto is "I control" and, it has to be said, you are a bit of a control freak, especially when it comes to relationships. You're the original bossy madam and won't take any nonsense from people – blokes especially – who won't do as they're told!

### If your Rising Sign is SAGITTARIUS

(♐), you're tall and slim, your face is oval, and your expression is open and honest. Your hair is thick and wavy and is either red or very dark. You have bright eyes, arched eyebrows and a smattering of freckles. Sagittarius rules the hips and, in other people's eyes, there's no one hipper (or hippier in some cases!) than you! You may see yourself as a cautious person, but others think you're 100 per cent reckless! Surprisingly (not to you, perhaps, but to others), the Sagittarius motto is "I think" and, contrary to popular belief, thinking is something you spend a lot of time doing. With regard to boys, as far as you're concerned, a date's a date (and usually a total riot if you've got anything to do with it!), but getting involved in a proper relationship requires much thought. You may be seen as crazy but you're not crazy enough to hurl yourself in at the deep end of love . . .

**If your Rising Sign is CAPRICORN (♑),** you're small and slim with a boyish air. You have thin, straight hair – dark most probably – a long face and a serious demeanour. Capricorn rules the teeth and the skeleton – perhaps that's why other people see you as someone who, once you've got your teeth into something, is like a dog with a bone! And you make no bones about letting other people see the real you either, the only difference between your opinion and theirs being that they see you as a rather sweet person. You're pretty hard on yourself, but that sort of modesty makes others warm to you. The Capricorn motto is "I learn" and that's something you do every minute of the day, especially with regard to relationships. Romantically, you aren't the sort who leaps at the chance of going out with the first bloke who fancies you: in fact, until you *really* have a boy's trust, you'll play hard to get . . .

**If your Rising Sign is AQUARIUS (♒),** you're very attractive with big eyes, a slightly "Roman" nose, a sharp chin and a sexy smile. You're tall and slim with long legs, narrow hips and a small bust. Aquarius rules the veins and the blood – very apt because no one likes to circulate more than you! You have loads of friends and you can somehow be someone different to each of them. You need different people for different reasons and not all the people you

meet and get to know realize this. So people are often surprised when they discover that there's more to you than initially meets the eye. The Aquarian motto is "I adapt" and, it's true, you can be a complete chameleon when you need to be – socially and more so when it comes to relationships. This can confuse some blokes – especially when you jump from one personality to another! – but others (a special few, admittedly) find this a most endearing quality . . .

**If your Rising Sign is PISCES (♓),** you have huge glittery eyes and a figure to die for. You're easy to spot because, although you always manage to look cool, you're such a scruff: if the hem of your skirt's hanging down or buttons are missing from your shirt, you're definitely a Pisces Rising girl! Pisces rules the feet and it's no secret that you're always opening your mouth and putting your trotter in it! Generally, you're seen as someone who couldn't really care less what others think of her. But that's not entirely true (you wouldn't be reading this if it was, would you?) and your main reason for appearing that way is because you don't want people to think it's up to them to build up your self-esteem. The Piscean motto is "I believe", making you very trusting, gullible even. Many a bloke has won your heart by spouting a load of old romantic codswallop and you, like a true Pisces Rising, have fallen for it. Better luck next time; and there *will* be a next time, don't doubt it for a second . . .

## The Taurus + Rising Sign Combinations
*The combination of your Sun Sign – Taurus – with your Rising Sign is very important when it comes to your attitude towards the opposite sex.*

If, for example, your **Rising Sign** is **Aries** and your Sun Sign is Taurus, you're the sort of person who rushes headlong into romance. Then, when things go wrong, you wonder why . . . Slow down a bit.

If you're a double Taurean – with a **Taurus Rising Sign** *and* a Taurus Sun Sign – your possessive streak is strong and may get in the way of a successful love life. So chill out a bit.

A **Gemini Rising Sign** combined with a Taurus Sun Sign means you love the thrill of romance and are always seeking to make it as exciting as possible. Secret love affairs will get you into no end of trouble.

A **Cancer Rising Sign** combined with a Taurus Sun Sign means you need to be in love at all costs – but it often costs you more than you expect.

A **Leo Rising Sign** combined with a Taurus Sun Sign makes you passionate and affectionate but not discerning enough. Your love life will improve when you get more selective.

A **Virgo Rising Sign** combined with a Taurus Sun Sign means that you put boyfriends and potential boyfriends on a pedestal – but don't forget, no one's perfect.

A **Libra Rising Sign** combined with a Taurus Sun Sign means you're a real game player and a tease. You like to keep blokes dangling on a string while you "um and ah" over just who you're going to choose (you wicked person, you!)

A **Scorpio Rising Sign** combined with a Taurus Sun Sign makes you most unlike a faithful Taurean: in fact, you're a top two-timer! (Yikes!)

A **Sagittarius Rising Sign** combined with a Taurus Sun Sign means there'll be many "loves" in your life, but only a few of them will mean anything to you.

A **Capricorn Rising Sign** combined with a Taurus Sun Sign suggests that you like the idea of long-term love, but find it hard to get a relationship going. You will find love but must be patient.

An **Aquarius Rising Sign** combined with a Taurus Sun Sign makes you extremely loyal: once you fall in love it could well be for ever. Aw!

A **Pisces Rising Sign** combined with a Taurus Sun Sign means you find the opposite sex totally irresistible. But falling in love as often as you do is just plain daft!

# The Secret Life Of Taurus

*Everyone knows the characteristics of their star sign, but we all have hidden depths. Check out yours . . .*

You're reliable, patient, determined, down-to-earth and strong-willed. The "salt of the earth", some might say. But there's also another, rather more frivolous side to your nature. You love music and parties, and you know how to have fun. You're a top host: anyone invited to a party at your gaff will be in for a great time – the music will be hot, the company fun and the munchies simply out of this world. No soggy crisps and stale peanuts for you – you'll have something really special laid on. You may not be the wittiest of conversationalists, but your quiet charm guarantees you a whole load of admirers. And although you tell everyone that the quiet life's for you and you don't mind the everyday tedium of life (in fact, sometimes you insist that you actually enjoy a nice routine!), you secretly yearn for excitement. The thing is, it often takes a more adventurous, risk-taking friend to bring this element out in you.

**Strengths:** You want the best and you're prepared to wait as long as it takes to get it. Your timing is excellent and you're always in the right place at exactly the right time. You're a solid, reliable type, so people trust you as well as like you, especially as you're able to see things from a very practical perspective. You're a fighter too – start something and you always finish it.

**Weaknesses:** Your self-esteem is a bit on the low side and this can cause you to be lazy. Sometimes you can't be bothered to start a project because you believe it's going to fail. You also regard luxuries as necessities. Be honest now – do you really need the crusts cut off your sandwiches *every* time? A creature of habit, you tend to watch the clock a bit too much and if things don't happen when you expect them to, you're completely thrown out of sync.

**Fears:** You're really worried – neurotic almost – about timetables and schedules, and hate the thought of missing anything. Your other fear is of being angry. That's why you tend to bottle up so much. It's not good for you to be so controlled – try letting go sometimes. No one will think ill of you – they may even admire you for it.

**Desires:** Although you'd never let on, all you really, really want is an easy life, a huge bed, loads of delicious grub and to be permanently pampered! Thing is, it costs money to live like this – another of your great desires. You can never have enough of the stuff.

**Secret talent:** Painting (don that beret and wield that palette!) You don't come across as an arty type – people think you're just too down-to-earth and practical – but beauty moves you in a deeply powerful way. And, being a sensualist, you love the idea of slapping rich oils on canvas. If you have a secret yen to paint, never mind your mates' surprise, just do it. Salvador Dali, the famous Spanish artist, was a Taurus.

**As a girlfriend . . .** you're loyal, devoted and loving – not to mention sensuous and romantic. What more could a boy want? Well, possibly to feel a bit less crowded. Problem is, once you decide you like someone, you want them to spend all their time with you – and when that isn't possible you want to know just what they're up to. The lad in question may find this a tad claustrophobic and you might be in danger of scaring him off. Show him you care by all means, but give him some space too.

**As a best friend . . .** they don't come much better than you. Your best mate will really appreciate the no-nonsense, practical way you see things. However, there's a chance she may also feel a little frustrated with you at times – especially if she likes life to be one long buzz and doesn't understand a creature of habit who likes her comforts. But this won't spoil your friendship with her – you're too loyal to drop a mate just because she doesn't understand you . . .

# Taurus In Love

## Emotional Taurus

You take your time choosing a suitable partner, but once you've found someone you like, you're happy to stay with them for a very long time. You have a great need for security and like to be in a relationship mainly for this reason. Although you like being part of a cosy twosome, you do find it difficult to open up totally and be yourself within an intimate relationship. It's not easy for you to admit that you've fallen in love and, when you feel yourself falling, you'll do your utmost to convince yourself (and the guy you've fallen for) that it's not really happening. This is just a form of self-protection as you're so scared of being hurt. For the same reason, you project a tough and independent image and like your partner to think that this is the Real You. But, unless he's particularly thick-skinned, it's highly unlikely that he'll believe that you're like that all the time.

**Advice:** * Don't keep that soft, sensitive side hidden away. Being soft doesn't mean being weak, so don't

worry about appearing too clingy. * Let yourself go and let the boy you love know that you're human!

## Practical Taurus

Taurean females really aren't happy on their own – more than anything, they love the idea of living happily ever after as half of a couple. When you do get into the domestic set-up of your dreams, you're likely to spend a lot of time, effort and money on keeping up appearances. You like your mates to regard you as settled and mature, and what better way to achieve this than by being in a long-term relationship? Because of this attitude, many Taurean girls get engaged or married early in the belief that they'll get more respect if they appear more grown-up. They usually find, however, that this action doesn't have the desired effect. Problems may arise when you become more interested in being a couple and doing coupley things than in your bloke himself, and when you get that cosy, you lose your adventurous streak and your urge to go out.

**Advice:** * Don't grow old before your time: there's plenty of time for that. * Don't stick in a relationship just because you don't want to be single. Stay in it because you actually like the bloke. * Realize that you can be seen as mature and settled even if you're not part of a twosome. Try it and see . . .

## Taurean Love Crises

You come across as very practical when it comes to romance and seem to be perfectly aware that love is rarely problem-free. That's why you're usually well-prepared to deal with any eventualities, knowing (though not at all in a defeatist way) that this sort of thing (whatever it might be) was bound to happen sooner or later. Despite this rather sensible outlook, you're absolutely terrified of being let down and this, combined with the fact that you're so patient and loving, means you'll do anything you can to keep your relationship going, even allowing your partner to get away with metaphorical murder in the meantime. Having said that, even if it's your partner who causes the problems in your relationship, you can often make matters worse by seeking solace elsewhere (often in another guy's arms). The main crises, however, arise from your own possessiveness.

**Advice:** * Learn to relax. * Don't always expect the worst from your bloke. * No matter how close you are to your boyfriend, try to remember that you don't actually own him.

## In short . . .

**They Love You . . .** because you're sweet, reliable and straightforward. But it's your beauty, charm and laid-back nature which make you initially so very attractive. And, once a guy gets to know you, he'll discover that your thoughtfulness, generosity and sincerity – not to mention your sexiness – are a positive bonus.

**They Leave You . . .** because although you're faithful, loyal and attentive, you can overdo it and become horribly clingy, possessive and jealous. You're stubborn, too, and could try the patience of a saint with your dilly-dallying. When riled, your nasty temper explodes and can be quite scary. Also, the way you keep drawing attention to what you consider to be your bad points can be off-putting.

**When You Fall In Love . . .** you like to take things slowly. You're not the sort to fall head over heels in love because you need to get to know someone well before you can make any sort of commitment.

Check this Taurean compatibility chart to discover who you're likely to have a crush on, who you tend to date, who you fall in love with, and who's best kept as a friend. Check the key for ratings.

| His Sign | You'd have a CRUSH on . . . | You tend to DATE . . . | You could LOVE . . . | You're just good FRIENDS with . . . |
|---|---|---|---|---|
| Aries | | | | ❀ |
| Taurus | | | ▶ | |
| Gemini | ❤ | | | |
| Cancer | ▶ | ❀ | ❤ | ▶ |
| Leo | | ❤ | ❀ | ❤ |
| Virgo | | ▶ | | |
| Libra | ❤ | | | |
| Scorpio | ❤ | | ❀ | |
| Sagittarius | ❀ | | | |
| Capricorn | | | | ▶ |
| Aquarius | | | | ❤ |
| Pisces | | | | |

Key: ❤ = In a major way  ❀ = When you're in the mood  ▶ = In a minor way

27

# Which Taurus Are You?

*As you already know, being born between April 20 and May 20 makes you a Taurus. But contrary to popular belief, there isn't just one type of Taurus. There are actually four. The one you are depends on your date of birth. Check below and see whether you're Miss Ambitious, Miss Control, Miss Sharing or Miss Natural . . .*

## Born April 20–26?
### You're MISS AMBITIOUS

Often known as Aries-Taurus Cusp and born close to the sign of Aries, you possess qualities of both signs. You're like an Aries in that you're fiery, smart and love new challenges but, like a Taurean, you're a little stubborn, but also sensual, intuitive and charming. Your personality is "bigger" than the average Taurean's and because of this you tend to be able to control the people around you. You like to do your own thing and don't react well when you're told what to do by someone else. You are hugely ambitious and, if you're not careful, your ambitions can take over your life. As with every "cusp" personality, you're a mass of contradictions – one minute, you're totally mad-for-it, and the next minute you'd rather just lay back and see what happens.

## Born April 27–May 6?
### You're MISS CONTROL

Your most obvious Taurean trait is your stubbornness. In fact, you're the most stubborn of all Taureans and this is down to the fact that you're determined to have total control over your life. You *have* to do things your own way and if anyone tries to talk you into doing things their way – even if you know they're right – you'll only compromise after you've given your way a try first. If life goes according to plan, you're great to be around; when things go wrong, you get all morose and depressed. And it's while you're in this frame of mind that you become blinkered to everyone and everything, causing you to miss out on many opportunities. You're very concerned with material things, and like to be surrounded by beauty and comfort. Eating and sleeping are your fave pastimes.

## Born May 7–13?
### You're MISS SHARING

You're the most loving and giving of all the Taurean types and this goes towards explaining why you need a romantic interest in your life at all times. You're more talkative than the average Taurus and, because of this, you need the appreciation, love and listening skills of other folk. Many performers are born into this category (Bono from U2, Harry Enfield,

Natalie from All Saints and Sinead from B*Witched to name but a few), all of whom love an audience. You're a philosophical type: the stuff you say seems to stick in the minds of others and, in turn, makes them think. You enjoy spouting your opinions, but when you overdo it you may be accused of taking yourself too seriously. You're a leader, but in quite an unconventional, unobvious way.

## Born May 14–20?
## You're MISS NATURAL

You're always going on about how important it is to be yourself, which is odd because, of all the Taurean types, you're the most inhibited! Once you learn how to shake off these inhibitions (and, in time, you will), you can be as natural as you want to be. You hate complications and confrontations: all you want is an easy life. Despite this, you're pretty tough, can cope better than most with criticism and, even though you're aware of your insecurities, you manage to hide them well. You really appreciate natural behaviour in others and resent anyone who deliberately tries to be something they're not. You adore animals and love children (probably due to the fact that they're so natural), but in wanting to be like them you can sometimes come across as a bit naive.

# Part 2:

# Looks

*It's often easy to identify a person's star sign by their looks and physique. In this chapter you'll find a description of the typical appearance of a Taurus. If this doesn't quite fit, however, it doesn't necessarily mean you're not a typical Taurus – it simply means that other factors, including your Rising Sign (see pages 6–19), have influenced your image. Sometimes, the combination of your Rising Sign and your Sun Sign gives you a more "mixed" look. So don't be alarmed if it doesn't sound like you. You're just that bit more intriguing!*

# Taurus – The Natural Wonder!

As a Taurus, you have a kind of earthy look about you. This simply means you look sensual in a gorgeously natural way. Other people warm to you because of your looks – you look approachable and not at all scary (unless you're Cher, that is, a Taurean whose natural beauty has been altered somewhat by extensive cosmetic surgery!).

Most Taurean females have long and very curvy figures (whether you're a chubby or slim Taurean depends on your eating habits). Whether you're short or tall (and, again, Taureans come in both varieties!), you have a solid look about you. Your shoulders are high and square, your hips and bums may be wide, but your waist is tiny! Your legs are good – usually long and muscular – and your feet are long and broad.

**Top tip:** Instead of trying to hide what you consider to be a big bot (!), make the most of your good features instead.

If you want to find out more about your body – and compare your looks to those of the other eleven signs – check the chart opposite . . . (But remember that some of you won't have the typical looks for your sign.)

Body Beautiful? Check the chart below and find out . . .

| Your Sign | Height-wise you're . . . | Build-wise you're . . . . | Best feature is your . . . | Worst feature is your . . . | You come across as . . . | You'd be fit if you weren't . . . |
|---|---|---|---|---|---|---|
| TAURUS | medium/tall | sturdy | neck | shoulders | cuddly | lazy |
| GEMINI | short/medium | slight | arms | skin | small and cute | faddy |
| CANCER | short/medium | chunky | skin | chest | soft | such a hypochondriac |
| LEO | short | slim but solid | posture | ankles | tough | arrogant |
| VIRGO | medium/tall | slender | legs | nails | clean | fussy |
| LIBRA | medium | curvy | waist | bum | sexy | indecisive |
| SCORPIO | medium | stocky | bum | legs | strong | self-destructive |
| SAGITTARIUS | medium/tall | athletic | thighs | hips | very fit | impatient |
| CAPRICORN | short | small | ankles | knees | earthy | fatalistic |
| AQUARIUS | tall | strong | hands | calves | unusual | unwilling |
| PISCES | short | thickset | chest | feet | warm | self-pitying |
| ARIES | medium/tall | big-boned | shoulders | scar/s(?!) | big and bold | accident prone |

# Fit For Anything!

**W**hen it comes to getting and keeping fit, Taureans *mean* well but . . . it's just so hard to get away from the TV some-times . . . And the sofa . . . well . . . it's just *sooo* comfy. And it's cold out there . . . Basically, you're a tad lazy and would come up with any excuse rather than go for a workout. Also, because you're a slow mover with a slow metabolism, you have a tendency to put on weight quickly and easily and, instead of this making you want to do something about it, you're more likely to go into denial and pretend it isn't happening. The perfect exercise for you is dancing, but not at home with your Walkman on – at a dance class, where someone's keeping an eye on you, making sure you're doing what you're supposed to be doing.

**Top tip:** Ruled by Venus, you're a lover of beauty so your appearance is important to you. When exercising, keep telling yourself how gorgeous you're going to look afterwards – that should keep you going!

If you want to find out more about your health – and also see how fit the other eleven signs are – check the chart opposite . . .

Find out how to stay on top form by referring to this chart . . .

| Your Sign | The most vulnerable part of your body | Most frequent illness | You have accidents . . . | Stay healthy by . . . |
|---|---|---|---|---|
| **TAURUS** | throat | sore throats | because of your clumsiness | eating healthily |
| **GEMINI** | arms and hands | coughs | because you get so stressed out | doing yoga |
| **CANCER** | chest | indigestion | because you get so tired | improving your diet |
| **LEO** | back | backache | because you are always showing off | expressing yourself |
| **VIRGO** | stomach | tummy ache | because you're always so tense | relaxing more |
| **LIBRA** | kidneys | urinary infections | because you overdo it | exercising more |
| **SCORPIO** | reproductive organs | menstrual problems | with hot things | not ignoring problems |
| **SAGITTARIUS** | hips and thighs | feeling run-down | when playing sport | calming down a bit |
| **CAPRICORN** | knees | colds | because you work too hard | working less |
| **AQUARIUS** | calves and ankles | allergies | with your ankles | slowing down |
| **PISCES** | feet | being generally unwell | because your head's in the clouds | staying alert |
| **ARIES** | head | headaches | with sharp things | working out |

# Fashion Victim? Only If It Doesn't Cost Too Much . . .

Although you're quite interested in fashion, you're more concerned with being comfortable than with looking like a supermodel. You enjoy shopping for clothes, but don't like spending too much on them. That doesn't mean you like looking a slob: you prefer pretty dresses and feminine clothes in your favourite colours – mint green, powder blue and baby pink. And dainty shoes and sandals are a must! You're not overly wacky with your clothes and, although you like to look good, you don't like to attract an unnecessary amount of attention. You like well-cut, not too tight clothes in soft, natural fabrics.

**Top Tip:** Try to avoid fussy styles, wearing too many clothes at once (you love a few layers!), and over-accessorizing.

For more details about what you wear and how you wear it – and to check out how stylish the other eleven signs are – see the chart opposite . . .

More about clothes on the chart below . . . .

| Your Sign | Your clothes must be . . . | The colour that suits you best is . . . | Your best thing to wear is a . . . | Your fave fabric is . . . | Favourite shop |
|---|---|---|---|---|---|
| TAURUS | comfortable | blue | scruffy pair of jeans | denim | Millets |
| GEMINI | fashionable | yellow | sexy slip-dress | silk | Knickerbox |
| CANCER | feminine | sea green | long and girlie dress | lace | Benetton |
| LEO | noticeable | orange | tiara | lurex | Morgan |
| VIRGO | clean | white | pair of pinstripe trousers | cotton | Marks & Spencer |
| LIBRA | flirty | lilac | little A-line skirt | satin | Miss Selfridge |
| SCORPIO | sexy | black | pair of skintight trousers | leather | French Connection |
| SAGITTARIUS | sporty | turquoise | wet suit! | rubber | Any sports shop |
| CAPRICORN | smart | brown | cool skirt suit | linen | Wallis |
| AQUARIUS | original | bright blue | slinky bikini | lycra | Miss Selfridge |
| PISCES | pretty | grey | pair of platforms | velvet | Shelly's |
| ARIES | a statement | red | fab hat | wool | Accessorize |

# Tasty Taurus!

**Y**our most noticeable features are your large eyes with their steady gaze, your pouty mouth and your tiny ears. You have a roundish face and a lovely complexion (which isn't so lovely when you're stressed or upset – that's when it comes out in blotches!). A wide forehead is characteristic of the sign, as is a squarish jawline. Taurean hair is often fine but abundant, and often curly or frizzy. And, like the bull that rules your sign, you may have curls that hang low over your forehead!

**Top tip:** You may find your hair hard to care for and it can get unruly. Because of this, it looks best completely cropped, plaited or dreadlocked, or teased into sleek and shiny curls with masses of hair products.

If you want to find out more about the top end of your body, take a peek at the chart opposite and, while you're there, check out the other eleven signs too!

Check out your face and hair on this special chart . . .

| Your Sign | Your hair is great because it's . . . | On a bad-hair day it's . . . | Your face shape is . . . | Your eyes are . . . | Your mouth is . . . | Your skin is . . . |
|---|---|---|---|---|---|---|
| TAURUS | soft | a total riot! | rounded | baby-big | pouty | clear |
| GEMINI | extreme | out of control! | oval | twinkly | always moving! | a pain! |
| CANCER | gorgeously girlie | messy to the max! | round | small | smiley | soft |
| LEO | your crowning glory! | a bit OTT | square-jawed | almond-shaped | thin-lipped | dry |
| VIRGO | squeaky clean! | lank | long | heavy-lidded | narrow | combination |
| LIBRA | thick | unmanageable | heart-shaped | big and pale | perfect! | smooth |
| SCORPIO | abundant | floppy | broad | penetrating | sexy | normal |
| SAGITTARIUS | shiny | flyaway | oblong | wide apart | huge! | freckly |
| CAPRICORN | heavy | greasy | narrow | sleepy-looking | downturned | oily |
| AQUARIUS | sleek | fine | wide | sparkly | big | sensitive |
| PISCES | silky | sparse-looking | babyish | massive! | doll-like | translucent |
| ARIES | strong | frizzy | square | dark | small | ruddy |

# Give Yourself A Make-Over!

When it comes to making the most of your facial character-istics, make-up can play a part. In astrology, beauty has a strong connection to the elements – Fire, Earth, Air and Water. Taurus is an Earth sign, which means you prefer a subtle, natural look. Check the characteristics of an Earth sign below (you share these with the two other Earth signs – Virgo and Capricorn), then give yourself an elementary make-over . . .

## As an EARTH sign, you:
- Are sexy but subtle
- Are sensual, sensitive and very touchy-feely
- Are down-to-earth, hard-working, practical and reliable
- Have a great sense of humour
- Love all the good things in life
- Can be bossy
- Hate anyone saying "no" to you
- Could never be unfaithful
- Take life and love pretty seriously

You've got a pretty face and are very good at making the most of it. By day, go without make-up apart from a bit of concealer stick on any blemishes or blotches you might have, a stroke of mascara in the same colour as your lashes and lightly coloured lips in a colour not far removed from your natural lip colour. At night, push the boat out with foundation, translucent powder and bolder eyeshadow in shades of brown, amber and beige.

**Top tips:** Avoid acid brights as they can drain your face and make you look quite ill. Line your lips with a dark brown pencil and fill in with a bold, nutty-coloured lipstick. Add lip gloss for that kiss-me party look.

# Part 3:
# Boy Stuff

# Quiz: Who's Your Star Guy?

*A lot has been said on the subject of cosmic compatibility, but you may have found that, although you're supposed to be attracted to a particular sign, you just keep going for the "wrong" ones.*

This isn't because you're a glutton for punishment – in fact, you may even discover that you get on quite well with these so-called incompatible signs – but is the result of how all the planets were positioned in the heavens at the time of your birth. Although you're a Taurean, there might have been more planets present in another sign – say, Gemini, for example – on the day you were born, causing you to take on more of the characteristics of that sign, and making you more attracted to Fire and Air signs than a typical Taurean would be. It takes an experienced astrologer to work out an individual's birth chart (and nearly everyone's chart is different), but doing this quiz is a simple way of working out which sign is most compatible with **you**, as opposed to your sign. Try it and see . . .

*1. Four different boys have the serious hots for you. They're all quite different in appearance. On looks alone, which one would you choose to go out with?*

a) Serious expression, medium height with a compact physique
b) Bright-eyed, slim with a cute grin
c) Muscly bod with long limbs, amazing eyes and sexy lips
d) Athletic and masculine-looking with striking facial features and fab hair

**2. At a party, you've made it clear that you fancy the guy who's standing alone on the other side of the room. Which course of action would you like him to take?**
a) Ask you to dance
b) Smile encouragingly but wait for you to make the first move
c) Show his intentions through body language and meaningful stares
d) Act as cool as he can, to make it a bit more challenging for you

**3. You finally get chatting. After a while, it becomes clear that he's more than keen. What happens next?**
a) You ask him back to your place
b) He suggests going on somewhere else
c) He snogs you suddenly and passionately
d) Nothing – you're both too shy

**4. What sort of clothes would you prefer a bloke to wear on your first date?**
a) Anything that suits him
b) Anything fashionable
c) Something sporty or casual but cool-looking

d) A shirt, jacket and trousers in natural fabrics or a smart suit

### 5. He's taking you out for a meal. Where?
a) Pizza Express
b) McDonald's
c) At a riverside café
d) An "as much as you can eat" carvery

### 6. As a date, he's . . .
a) Intense, serious and a little bit shy
b) Great – he really knows how to do and say all the right things, but seems to expect a lot in return
c) Talkative, unpredictable, a great laugh
d) A great listener, romantic, giving and considerate

### 7. Where would you like to go on your second date?
a) Round to his place to eat a takeaway and watch TV
b) To a party or wild nightclub
c) To the cinema or theatre
d) For a picnic in the country

### 8. What's your attitude towards marriage?
a) It's silly, outmoded and impractical – you can't ever imagine wanting to be married
b) It stops you being yourself – and until you're convinced otherwise you're happy to stay single
c) It's lovely – romantic and secure – you can't wait to walk up that aisle
d) It's a good idea for two people who really love each other to make a commitment – when you meet the right person, you'll definitely tie the knot

### 9. What, to you, would be the perfect holiday?

a) A real action holiday – pony-trekking, mountaineering or something like that

b) As long as there's a reasonable amount of luxury and you can spend time relaxing, you don't care where you go

c) Anywhere you can sample a bit of culture, unusual food and drink and feel all the more enlightened for it

d) Somewhere that stimulates your imagination and leaves you feeling mentally refreshed

### 10. Which colour is your favourite?

a) Bright yellow, violet or electric blue

b) Bright red, orange, gold or turquoise

c) Pale blue, pink, any shade of green, navy, brown or white

d) Grey, pale blue, silver, dark red, black or sea green

**Now work out your scores, making a note of how many F's, E's, A's and W's you get . . .**

1. a – E;  b – A;  c – W; d – F
2. a – F;  b – E;  c – W; d – A
3. a – W; b – A;  c – F;  d – E
4. a – W; b – A;  c – F;  d – E
5. a – A;  b – F;  c – W; d – E
6. a – E;  b – F;  c – A;  d – W
7. a – E;  b – F;  c – A;  d – W
8. a – A;  b – F;  c – W; d – E
9. a – F;  b – E;  c – A;  d – W
10. a – A;  b – F;  c – E;  d – W

**If you scored mostly F,** go to the FIRE section.
**If you scored mostly E,** go to the EARTH section.
**If you scored mostly A,** go to the AIR section.
**If you scored mostly W,** go to the WATER section.

(In the event of a "tie" – i.e., you score equally on two or more sections – you can go to both or all sections indicated and be ultimately equally attracted to two or more different star signs.)

# Fire

*Fire sign guys are:*
* Energetic
* Warm
* Fun-loving
* Passionate
* Enthusiastic
* A little bit crazy

*Sound like your type? Now answer this simple question:*

### Which of the following statements do you most agree with?

a)  When I go on a date, I like a guy to be spontaneous and passionate. If he wants more than a goodnight peck on the cheek that's just fine by me.

b) When I go out with a guy, I like to be treated with a substantial amount of respect. I like to have fun, but I hate being rushed and like to take relationships one step at a time.

c) All I want from a boyfriend is a good time. If he's

happy, I'm happy. I've no intentions of getting heavy with a guy – that's the best way to send him running.

*If you answered a) the guy for you is an **Aries**. To find out more about him, turn to page 51.*

*If you answered b) the guy for you is a **Leo**. To find out more about him, turn to page 62.*

*If you answered c) the guy for you is a **Sagittarius**. To find out more about him, turn to page 72.*

# Earth

**Earth sign guys are:**
* Hard-working
* Faithful
* Practical
* Loyal
* Down-to-earth
* A little bit sensible

*Sound like your type? Now answer this simple question:*

**Which of the following qualities do you believe to be the most important in a boyfriend?**

a) Serious sexiness
b) A fab sense of humour
c) Immense cleverness

*If you answered a) the guy for you is a **Taurus**. To find out more about him, turn to page 54.*

*If you answered b) the guy for you is a **Virgo**. To find out more about him, turn to page 64.*

*If you answered c) the guy for you is a **Capricorn**. To find out more about him, turn to page 75.*

# Air

*Air sign guys are:*
* Talkative
* Sociable
* Changeable
* Unpredictable
* Interesting
* A little bit "bonkers"

*Sound like your type? Now answer this simple question:*

### Which of the following dates would you prefer?

a) Going to a posh restaurant for dinner, then to see your fave band, then to the best nightclub in town to rave until the early hours.

b) Spending a day in the country, having a snog in a cornfield, followed by supper at an Olde Worlde Inne and a romantic train ride home, watching the sunset through the dusk.

c) Having a champagne breakfast (OK, so you may be under eighteen, but this is fantasy-land here) in a hot air balloon, a nice walk by the river, then on to see a fascinating film at your local cinema.

*If you answered a) the guy for you is a **Gemini**. To find out more about him, turn to page 56.*

*If you answered b) the guy for you is a **Libra**. To find out more about him, turn to page 67.*

*If you answered c) the guy for you is an **Aquarius**. To find out more about him, turn to page 78.*

# Water

*Water sign guys are:*
* Sensitive
* Sentimental
* Mysterious
* Secretive
* Intense
* A little bit weird

*Sound like your type? Now answer this simple question:*

**Which of the following holidays would you like best?**

a) A relaxing holiday by the sea, somewhere peaceful, picturesque and romantic.

b) A luxurious holiday in a historical setting, where there are lots of old ruins and places to explore.

c) A sailing holiday in a faraway, beautiful, uncrowded and exotic place.

*If you answered a) the guy for you is a **Cancer**. To find out more about him, turn to page 59.*

*If you answered b) the guy for you is a **Scorpio**. To find out more about him, turn to page 70.*

*If you answered c) the guy for you is a **Pisces**. To find out more about him, turn to page 80.*

# Astro-Boys

*So you've found your ideal romantic partner . . .
Well, now's the time to check him out good and
proper.*

## Aries (March 20–April 19)

He's a hero . . . because he's
really popular and has a zillion
mates you can flirt with. Also . . .
* He's honest and straightforward
* He's very affectionate
* He's sexy to the max
* He loves to spring little surprises
  on you
* Everyone thinks he's fab
* He's a top snogger!!

He's a zero . . . when he acts creepy
around girls (he could smarm for
Britain!) and two-times (sometimes
three-times) girlfriends. Plus . . .
* He's just too bossy
* He's always ogling other girls
* He tells the occasional "white" lie
* He's a bit of a stirrer
* He won't wait for anyone or anything
* He'll never love you more than he loves himself

## Personality Alert!

No matter how much he likes you, you'll never be his number one priority. Because his number one priority is (as if you haven't guessed) . . . himself!

**He looks great . . .** because he's got a fab body – not an ounce of fat! – a chiselled, model-like face and a sexy expression. He's slim and muscular with wide shoulders and snakey hips. Arien males usually have thick, dark, well-styled hair which they're always touching. Facially, they look much like the animal that represents their sign – a ram! – especially in profile, with a long straight nose, chiselled cheekbones, beetly eyebrows and small mouth and chin. He likes fashionable clothes in bright colours and although he generally favours the sporty look, he will dress up smart if the occasion requires it.

**He's a state . . .** because he's a bit of a poseur and tends to overdo it with the "designer" labels. (Also, if you don't like the facial characteristics of a ram, then he may not be your cup of tea . . . )

**Meet him . . .**
– wherever there's a football.
– getting on down at the grooviest club in town.
– in McDonald's – on either side of the counter.

**Impress him by . . .** being totally upfront. If you fancy him, don't be shy: tell him. He'll love you for it! To catch his attention, wear something bright (in his team's colours preferably). If he compliments you, be grateful, but don't let him see you flirt with other guys – that's something he can't stand.

**If you can't be bothered to do the running . . .** then that won't be a problem. He loves the thrill of the chase, so once he gets wind of you fancying him, he'll be straight in there! He certainly doesn't beat around the metaphorical bush when it comes to chatting up girls, so chances are he'll just come and tell you if he fancies you (unfortunately, he'll also tell you just as loud and clear if he doesn't!) He's a great snogger – and he knows it – so he may just lunge for your lips before he's even spoken to you! Scary or what?!

**Keep him by . . .** never bossing him around (especially in front of his mates); being mega-appreciative when he's nice to you; telling him you love him at every opportunity; not flirting with other blokes; showing him what a totally cool and busy chick you are!

**Dump him when . . .** you find him snogging your best mate. (And you will.)

**Love match:** If you're a Leo, a Libran or a Sagittarian, you're putty in his hands!

**Top Arien totty:** Mark Hamilton (Ash), Damon Albarn, Linford Christie, Coree (Damage), Will Mellor, Robert Downey Jnr and Paul Nicholls.

# Taurus (April 20–May 20)

**He's a hero . . .** because of his loving, gentle nature. He's loyal to those he loves and, whether you're his mate or his girlfriend, he'll stand by you at all times. Also . . .

* He has masses of sex appeal (and doesn't even know it!)
* He'll listen to your problems all day and all night
* He's modest, kind and reliable
* He makes you go all quivery whenever he touches you
* He's very romantic

**He's a zero . . .** because he's the King Of Self-Indulgence and barely notices you exist sometimes! Plus . . .

* He's a bit of a couch potato
* His temper can get out of control
* He can't always keep up with you
* His moods are too much to take sometimes
* He can be self-obsessed
* He's hideously stubborn

## Personality Alert!

His worst nightmare comes true when you finally discover that, underneath it all, he is in fact very boring! Oh no!!

**He looks great . . .** because he's super-cuddly and mega-cute. And he's got a million woolly jumpers that he won't mind lending you (only when you're his girlfriend of course . . . ). He has a clear complexion, a sweet little mouth and gorgeous eyes. Most Taurus guys love clothes – and while they like the idea of looking trendy, they tend to dress down, preferring comfortable clothes in natural colours and fabrics. Show him a little something in Lycra and he'll run a mile!

**He's a state . . .** mainly because sometimes he just can't be bothered and, looks-wise, could give Swampy a run for his money! Also, he's a right old sloucher – it's sometimes hard to tell the difference between a Taurean bloke on a sofa and a sack of spuds!

**Meet him . . .**
- round at his place (he doesn't get out much!)
- round his mate's house (he rarely has more than one close male friend).
- in the local greasy caff (he really enjoys a good fry-up!)

**Impress him by . . .** enjoying lazing around as much as he does and taking the lead when it comes to getting physical. He's very tactile, so when you're there on the sofa with him, touch him at every opportunity. He likes girls who are relaxed and know how to have a good time. He's a bit worried about being boring and stupid though, so don't tease him in any way – especially in front of his mates. (Or should we say mate?!)

**If you can't be bothered to do the running . . .** you could have a problem. He's a shy guy at the best of times, so don't expect him to bowl you over with his bird-pulling tactics. If he so much as smiles at you across a crowded room, he thinks he's being pushy. He takes his time working out who he fancies, but once he's made up his mind, he'll make sure he's near you at all times, giving you the chance to make *your* move on *him*. Very subtle . . .

**Keep him by . . .** having a fab sense of humour; being open about your feelings; not taking the mickey out of him; not snogging or fighting him in public; giving him the time and space he needs, especially when it comes to making decisions.

**Dump him when . . .** he asks for his jumpers back.

**Love match:** If you're a Virgo, Scorpio or Capricorn, you're the girl for him.

**Top Taurean totty:** Jas Mann (Babylon Zoo), Jay Darlington (Kula Shaker), Harry Enfield, Lance (N-Sync), Emilio Estevez and Sean Conlon (5ive) .

# Gemini (May 21–June 20)
**He's a hero . . .** because he's a social chameleon and you can take him anywhere! He has opinions on every subject and loves a chat. He's also broad-minded, but PC at the same time. Also . . .

* He gets on with all your mates
* He's a real good laugh
* He's ever so romantic
* Life's never dull when he's around
* He's a big kid

**He's a zero . . .** because, as he's so easily bored, he can make you feel boring! He's moody to the max and can be horribly irritable. He also "forgets" dates and can be immature. Plus . . .
* He's too demanding
* He's totally unpredictable
* He won't stop flirting
* He thinks nothing of dating two (or even three) girls at a time
* He's a huge show-off

# Personality Alert!

He may look like butter wouldn't melt in his mouth, but he's the best liar in the zodiac. So be prepared to be foiled!

**He looks great . . .** because his tall, slim physique makes him look quite model-like. He has a sweet face, with twinkly eyes and a very naughty expression.

**He's a state . . .** because his sense of "style" (if you can call it that) leaves a lot to be desired. He loves to be trendy, but gets it totally wrong sometimes and ends up looking like a rather sad fashion victim. And what's with all the daft hats?! If any bloke makes you feel like calling the Fashion Police, it'll be Mr Gemini!

**Meet him . . .**
– at the trendiest hot spot in town.
– on a bus, train or plane.
– in a mobile phone showroom.

**Impress him by . . .** telling him you fancy him in five different languages (he likes clever – and straight-talking – chicks!) or asking him to help you with *The Times* crossword. And when you get chatting to him, make sure you laugh at all his jokes (even the totally surreal ones!) Once you've located him, you must play it as cool as he does. Never show your jealous side (if you've got one) and try to maintain an air of mystery.

**If you can't be bothered to do the running . . .** don't expect him to come running after you. This guy never makes much effort when it comes to pulling – mainly because he doesn't have to. His looks mean that you can't fail to notice him, but if he fancies you, he will use his ability to bewitch you from a distance, without saying a word. A Gemini boy can make you feel "drawn" to him and, no matter how shy you are, you'll suddenly find that you're the one doing all the work! Note: once in his clutches it may be hard to escape!

**Keep him by . . .** being very understanding (telepathic preferably!); staying faithful (even when he's not!);

putting up with his moods; spending most of your time together talking about him.

**Dump him when . . .** he stops returning your phone calls, and starts making up crap excuses about where he's been and what he's been doing.

**Love match:** He can only have a long-term relationship with Libran, Sagittarian or Aquarian girls.

**Top Geminian totty:** Lenny Kravitz, Johnny Depp, Noel Gallagher and Jason Brown (5ive).

# Cancer (June 21–July 22)

**He's a hero . . .** because, most of the time, he's kind, caring, sensitive and trustworthy. He also cooks a mean roast dinner! Also . . .

* He's mega-romantic
* He'll never let you down
* He really understands you
* He'll love you more than anyone has ever loved you
* He's honest and sincere
* He won't hear a bad word said against you

**He's a zero . . .** because he's mega-crabby, secretly compares his girlfriends to his mum (and it's unlikely

any of them will live up to *her* angelic image), and can be unbelievably selfish. Plus . . .

* He spoils all your fun
* He winds you up like nobody else
* He's a bit of a drama queen!
* He thinks he's always in the right
* He wants everyone to feel sorry for him all the time

# Personality Alert!

He can be clingier than cling film and twice as suffocating! Shaking him off could prove difficult.

**He looks great . . .** with his high cheekbones and charming smile. His clothes are generally pretty cool, and so they should be: they cost enough! He has a rather distinctive face with well-defined features and a friendly expression.

**He's a state . . .** when he takes the "baggy" look too far and the crotch of his jeans is hovering way below knee level! And, although he's probably slim, he's able to pile on the pounds easily – and, sometimes when he gets involved in a relationship, he lets himself go and gets to be a right old bloater!

**Meet him . . .**
– beside the seaside (or anywhere there's water really).
– in an amusement arcade (he loves computer games).
– at home, eating a slap-up tea.

**Impress him by . . .** telling him loads of intimate stuff about yourself and avoiding asking him any nosy questions about himself. Also, as Cancer boys love a snack, share your Rolos with him and he'll be yours for life!

**If you can't be bothered to do the running . . .** it could take some time before he'll chase you. He's a bit shy so he's not going to make the first move, no matter how many hints you give him. If he even vaguely suspects that you don't like him he'll run a mile. If you make the first move, he'll respond quickly and usually positively. Most Cancer guys, once they're sure of your feelings, can get very romantic and will try to woo you in all the traditional ways – with flowers, poetry, love letters . . . the works!

**Keep him by . . .** telling him you'll love him forever; being a total tower of strength; standing up for him even when you think he's in the wrong; always taking his opinions and his ideas seriously; being faithful; making him believe he can trust you.

**Dump him when . . .** he stops and gazes wistfully in the window of Ratners every time you go shopping!

**Love match:** When he settles, it'll be with a Scorpian, Capricornian or Piscean chick.

**Top Cancerian totty:** Jamie Redknapp, George Michael, Keith Duffy and Shane Lynch (Boyzone), Tom Cruise, Terry Caldwell (East 17), Prince William and Ross Kemp (EastEnders).

# Leo (July 23–August 22)

**He's a hero** . . . because he's manly, sexy and in control. He's also very generous and great fun to go out with. Also . . .

* He loves a good cuddle
* He buys you tons of pressies
* He's majorly optimistic
* He'll take good care of you
* He'll always forgive you

**He's a zero** . . . because he's a pain-in-the-butt show-off with an ego the size of Edinburgh! Plus . . .

* He's always telling you what to do
* He needs constant flattery
* He fancies himself more than he fancies you
* He's too demanding
* He expects you to drop all your mates in favour of him

## Personality Alert!

He can be totally embarrassing – especially when he insists on giving you massive snogs in public!

**He looks great** . . . as he's a fine figure of a lad with broad shoulders and lush hair. He may not be that lofty, but his posture is good and he strides around in a very "tall" and purposeful way. His face is unusual and usually has something feline about it – slightly slanty eyes perhaps . . . or whiskers maybe! (A lot of post-adolescent Leo guys favour a goatee beard!)

**He's a state . . .** because he wears too much jewellery (how many chains can a guy drape round one neck?), his hair is too coiffeured (à la The Bee Gees circa 1976), and his "look" is just a bit too considered (i.e. you can tell he spends hours in front of the mirror).

**Meet him . . .**
- at a gig (one where his band is playing).
- at the theatre (he'll be the star of the show).
- at the cash-point machine (he always has a good wad on him!).

**Impress him by . . .** flattering him all the time (it'll get you everywhere!) and by being totally committed, dependent even (he likes a girl who brings out the chauvinist in him!). Flattery gets you absolutely everywhere with this guy – no line is too corny! Compliment him on his clothes, his hair, his bike – anything! – and he'll be instantly smitten. He likes lively, upfront girls, so skulking around waiting for him to make the first move won't impress him. Oh – and if you want to make him yours, you should be supermodel gorgeous (although preferably slightly lower on the beauty scale than himself – he hates to be outshone!).

**If you can't be bothered to do the running . . .** he's sure as hell too proud to make a move on you. He's so wrapped up in himself, he won't have time to waste chasing girls. If he fancies you, he'll let you know in quite an obvious way but will then sit back and expect you to do all the running. His ego won't allow him to do it any other way!

**Keep him by . . .** being naturally beautiful (he doesn't ask for much, this guy); always paying your way (he's generous but hates being taken for granted); never criticizing him; being ready to party at the drop of a hat.

**Dump him when . . .** he starts telling you that, more than anything, you've always been a really good friend to him.

**Love match:** He'll find long-term love with a Sagittarian, Aquarian or Arien female.

**Top Leo totty:** Matt Le Blanc, Sean Moore (Manic Street Preachers), Arnie Schwarzenegger, Fatboy Slim, David Duchovny and Christian Slater.

# Virgo (August 23–September 22)

**He's a hero . . .** with a brilliant sense of humour – he's the wittiest sign of the zodiac – and a helpful, sympathetic and protective nature. Highly desirable. Also . . .

* He's very clever
* He's extremely cool
* He's never late
* He likes a laugh
* He's fussy about who he goes out with – if he's chosen you, you *must* be special!

**He's a zero . . .** because his analytical and critical nature can be off-putting. He can also be a bit grumpy and over-demanding. Plus . . .

* He's always putting you down
* He makes a right song and dance about everything you do
* He's a bit mean
* He thinks you're lucky to be in any way connected to him
* He rarely says anything nice to you
* He's emotionally repressed

## Personality Alert!
He can pick so many holes in you that you could feel like a colander by the end of your first date!

**He looks great . . .** with his bright eyes, faintly "amused" expression and spotlessly clean and immaculately ironed clothes. Virgo blokes are attractive – in their own quirky little way. Some look a bit delicate – all knees, elbows and knobbly bits! Most have narrow faces, bright eyes, long noses, thin lips, pointy chins and fine hair. He wears clean, well-pressed clothes in natural fabrics (such as cotton, wool and silk) – classy!

**He's a state . . .** only first thing in the morning. And even then, his 'jamas are only a teensy bit crumpled! His only other fashion crime is that he does seem to favour narrow-legged trousers and will insist on donning his "drainpipes" even when everyone else is flaunting their flares.

**Meet him . . .**
- in the supermarket (he's the one referring to a really long list).
- in the chemist's or health food shop (he's always got something wrong with him and in need of cures).
- in the hairdresser's (he has his hair trimmed at least twice a month!)

**Impress him by . . .** being a "quality bird" (he hates cheapness of any description) and not being coarse or over the top when attempting to pull him. Once you get chatting, don't laugh when he harps on about all his ailments (and he has lots); try to stay chirpy (if there's any moaning to be done, *he* wants to be the one doing it!); and make a point of being very (*very*) interested in everything he says.

**If you can't be bothered to do the running . . .** don't worry – as long as he's confident you like him, he'll have no qualms about making a move on you. If a Virgo bloke is trying to pull you, you may not notice at first – he's *that* subtle (some would say devious!) When chatting you up, he'll try all his best one-liners on you and have you in fits of laughter. Once he's got you hooked though, he gets really serious and, to some girls, this can be impressive in itself.

**Keep him by . . .** being 100 per cent devoted; allowing him to impress other girls with his witty quips (he's not flirting – honest!); never gossiping about him with your mates; being mega-sensitive when it comes to his feelings; not springing surprises on him.

**Dump him when . . .** you start to feel like one of his many ailments.

**Love match:** If he wants to meet his match, he should be looking for a Capricorn, Pisces or Taurus.

**Top Virgoan totty:** Keanu Reeves, Charlie Sheen, Hugh Grant, Paul Winterhart (Kula Shaker), Jarvis Cocker, Liam Gallagher and Jimmy Constable (911).

# Libra (September 23– October 22)

**He's a hero . . .** because he has very strong beliefs and is a great mediator. When you come over all "damsel in distress", he's the guy to save you.

Also . . .
* He's sensitive, sensual and sexy
* He'll tell you all the things you want to hear
* He's a great listener
* He's very polite
* He's great to go out with
* His moods are pretty constant
* He's pretty smart

**He's a zero . . .** because he's vain, superficial, manipulative and so charming he makes you feel sick sometimes. Plus . . .
* He flirts too much
* He's lazy

* He talks a right load of rubbish at times
* He's horribly indecisive
* He's *sooo* impractical
* He's a bit of a fibber

# Personality Alert!

He's a sneaky, smarmy snake-in-the-grass, who'll two-time you at the first opportunity. (Oh dear. And he seemed like such a nice chap . . . )

**He looks great** . . . because he's got dimples, a cheeky smile and a lovely pouty mouth. He looks after his clothes well – even his oldest trackie pants look brand new. His body is athletic-looking, his posture is good and his movements are graceful. He dresses to suit the occasion and can go from looking smart to scruffy, from frumpy to fashionable in a matter of hours. *Fact:* you can spot a Libran bloke by his shoes – he almost always wears baseball boots or trainers.

**He's a state** . . . because he's got such bad colour coordination, you'd need sunglasses to look at some of his "ensembles". And what's with the baseball cap – is it welded to his head or what?

**Meet him . . .**
– on a computer course.
– at an after-school/work discussion group.
– in the pet shop (he adores animals!)

**Impress him by** . . . telling him you're on intimate terms with Robbie Williams and most of All Saints (he loves a lig!), then inviting him to a celebrity bash. (It's not your fault if they all fail to turn up!) If you're interested in this bloke, then above all else you must be easy-going and intelligent. If you're daft or demanding, he won't want to know. He likes a girl to be independent so impress him by parpling on about your numerous extra-curricular activities and your bulging-at-the-seams social diary. To clinch the deal, compliment his looks and comment on his great wit and insight. He's a sucker for flattery!

**If you can't be bothered to do the running . . .** you won't have to wait long for him to come after you. He'll use his charm, good looks and generosity to attract your attention. He's an expert chatter-upper, so half the time you won't even know he's on the pull. He'll flatter you, be truly fascinated by everything you say and laugh his noggin off at all your jokes.

**Keep him by . . .** being caring and supportive; allowing him space for his own "interests" (this may or may not include dating other girls. Yikes!); having friends and hobbies of your own; being funny; paying him lots of compliments and springing lavish surprises on him.

**Dump him when . . .** the flowers he sends you start smelling of guilt.

**Love match:** He needs a girl who understands him – an Aquarian, Arien or Geminian perhaps.

**Top Libran totty:** Declan Donnelly, Brett Anderson (Suede), Will Smith and Zac (Zachary Walker) Hanson from Hanson.

## Scorpio (October 23–November 22)

**He's a hero** . . . because he's dynamic, caring and totally unshockable. And, although he's a perfectionist, he's remarkably understanding when it comes to other people's shortcomings. Also . . .

* He's quick-witted and clever
* He can give you everything you need
* He'll really look after you
* He makes you believe he knows you better than you know yourself
* He's got a sexy and mysterious aura
* He can help you get whatever you want

**He's a zero** . . . because his overwhelming need to be in control can be scary. He's also capable of being hideously self-destructive if things don't go his way. Plus . . .

* He's capable of being dangerously possessive
* He's at the mercy of that green-eyed monster
* He wants to know everything about you but tells you very little about himself
* He thinks he's never wrong
* He makes out he's a real one-woman guy, but he can be unfaithful on a whim

## Personality Alert!

He's such a control freak, he'll have you on a dog lead

and signed up for Crufts as soon as you can say "Yes, master (woof!)".

**He looks great . . .** thanks to those deeply gorgeous eyes and that intense stare. A Scorpio bloke can take on many outward appearances but he's usually casual-but-smartly dressed, well built (though not always tall), with broad shoulders and chest, little snakey hips and a cute butt! He's likely to have a wide forehead, a thick neck, bushy eyebrows and hairy arms(!) All very nice (if you like that kind of thing . . . )

**He's a state . . .** because sometimes he goes too far with the old macho image and ends up looking like a lumberjack! Plus . . . *Fact:* if a guy has bow-legs, chances are he's a Scorpio!

**Meet him . . .**
- on the rugby pitch (he loves a scrum or two!).
- in the bookshop, looking for a good thriller or detective novel.
- in bed, watching *Inspector Morse* videos.

**Impress him by . . .** finding out everything about him before you actually speak to him, then pretending you're psychic! This guy is pretty tricky to ensnare because he has extremely high expectations. He likes to do his own thing so won't necessarily be attracted to you simply because *you* like playing pool too. And anyway, he'd rather you were there in a cheerleader role than in a directly competitive one. If you can prove you're discreet, uncritical and not in the tiniest bit jealous, he *may* just give you a second glance.

**If you can't be bothered to do the running** ... that's not a problem – for a short while anyway. If he hears you have the hots for him, he'll be secretly flattered but won't be that obvious in his quest to pull you. His favourite pulling technique is staring. Then he'll take off his shades and stare some more. If that doesn't have the desired effect (i.e. you slavering over him in a matter of minutes), he'll forget all about you and move on to someone who's more receptive to his magnetism.

**Keep him by** . . . being faithful; being realistic rather than romantic; telling him you're the luckiest girl in the world (why? Because you're going out with him of course!); and never accusing him of being in the wrong (even when he is).

**Dump him when** . . . he starts blaming you for his self-destructive behaviour.

**Love match:** The only girls he's truly happy with are Pisceans, Taureans and Cancerians.

**Top Scorpian totty:** Alonza Bevan (Kula Shaker), Ethan Hawke, Leonardo DiCaprio, Ike (Clarke Isaac) Hanson from Hanson and Alex James (Blur).

# Sagittarius (November 23– December 21)

**He's a hero** . . . because he's honest and fair-minded, always sees the best in people and would never bear a grudge against anyone. He's also a genuinely

interesting person and is excellent
company. Also . . .
* He can always cheer you up
* He's never boring
* He's always got a smile on his face
* He's your best friend
* Nothing's dull when he's around

**He's a zero . . .** because he's impatient,
reckless and argumentative. And he's
always telling people how to run their
lives when it's *his* life – more than
anyone's – that needs sorting. Plus . . .
* He always seems to be putting his foot in it
* He's really immature
* You can't rely on him
* He can't sit still for a minute
* He's got a bit of an unpredictable temper
* He's incapable of being faithful

## Personality Alert!
He's about as easy to lean on as a cloud!

**He looks great . . .** but only by accident! When you
meet him, the first thing you'll notice is his gorgeous
legs and bum. If you can drag your eyes upwards, you
may notice his big mouth, sparkling eyes and cute little
hair "do".

**He's a state . . .** most of the time. In fact, even on a
good day, he looks as if he's covered his body in glue
and run backwards through his wardrobe! He's got

absolutely no dress sense and anything he wears is usually mismatched, crumpled or just plain grubby. What a scruff!

**Meet him . . .**
– dreamily reading the special offer cards in travel agents' windows.
– on holiday.
– at a wild party.

**Impress him by . . .** doing something pretty spectacular – it's the only way you'll ever get him away from the other girls. He likes girls who are as free and easy as he is, so if you're ready to do crazy, impulsive things at a moment's notice, you may be the girl for him. He's not keen on girls who are too grown-up, so coming on all sophisticated with him just won't work.

**If you can't be bothered to do the running . . .** he's more than happy to do it. He desperately needs to be liked and he'll do anything – including lie – to impress you. He'll try to be cool, but he's not. But his most successful tactic is playing the bumbling idiot – it works a treat every time and may even work on you!

**Keep him by . . .** telling him you're perfectly happy about having an "open" relationship; constantly reminding him that you've "never felt like this about anyone before" while at the same time not putting any restraints on him (tricky, eh?); inviting him on all your girls' nights out (he won't go but he'll appreciate being asked).

**Dump him when . . .** he says he's going away for the weekend, then disappears for three months.

**Love match:** If you're an Arien, Geminian or Leo you'll find this guy totally irresistible.

**Top Sagittarian totty:** Michael Owen, Ryan Giggs, Gary Lineker, Brad Pitt, Neil Codling (Suede) and Jamie Theakston.

# Capricorn (December 22–January 20)

**He's a hero . . .** because he's brave, realistic and is a great person to turn to for advice. Also, if you're feeling low, he's just the guy to give your ego a boost. Also . . .

* He's loyal
* He always lets you win arguments
* He'll never forget your birthday (or your mum's come to that!)
* You can talk to him about practically anything

**He's a zero . . .** because he's narrow-minded and refuses to see things from other people's points of view. And, although painfully modest on the surface, deep down he's a tad full of himself. Plus . . .

* He has an overdeveloped dark side (oo-er!)
* He tends to take things the wrong way

* He can be a bit predictable
* He's very insecure
* He won't take any risks
* He's a bit tight with his cash

## Personality Alert!

He could drive you mad with his incessant talk of computers!

**He looks great** . . . in his good-quality, expensive gear. He wears a lot of his fave colour – black. But he looks best when his girlfriend dresses him. Because he's a tad conservative, he doesn't particularly stand out, but once you're pointed in his direction, you'll realize how attractive he can be with his bright, intelligent-looking eyes and pixie-ish face.

**He's a state** . . . because he can't do a thing with his hair! It's stuck to his head like seaweed to a rock! It's unlikely that you'll be overwhelmed by this guy's looks, because although he's *kind* of cute, he's not what you'd call a "stunner". And why does he look so *worried* all the time?

**Meet him** . . .
– at the railway station (he's a closet trainspotter!).
– buying CDs (he's a tune-aholic – although he's more Bach than Backstreet!).
– in the library, studying for a "project" (he's such a swot!).

**Impress him by** . . . asking him how fax machines

work or asking him out by e-mail. (He loves girls with an interest in technology.) He likes quiet, sophisticated girls and won't be impressed by anyone loud, crude or raucous. So you can forget about telling him your fave dirty jokes! He likes you to be interested in his hobbies and won't take too kindly to any teasing.

**If you can't be bothered to do the running** . . . he's not a natural flirt so won't go out of his way to go after you. Most Capricorn guys favour the subtle approach and would rather get a mutual mate to introduce you than approach you. Once he's got your attention, he'll try to blind you with his vast intellect. If you're the type of girl who prefers brain to brawn, this just might work.

**Keep him by** . . . not yawning when he's talking technology; getting engaged on your first date (he likes to feel secure in a relationship); giving him privacy when he needs it; being quiet and refined; not moaning about his hobbies, even if he spends more time on them than he does on you.

**Dump him when** . . . you discover his little black book contains more than just the numbers of trains . . .

**Love match:** If you're a Taurean, a Virgoan or a Cancerian, get on in there!

**Top Capricornian totty:** Denzel Washington, Tim (Ash), Jim Carrey and Gary Barlow.

# Aquarius (January 21– February 18)

**He's a hero . . .** because he's loyal and deep-thinking. He finds people fascinating and is incredibly observant. If you've got any questions about human behaviour, he's the guy to ask! Also . . .

* He's amusing
* He never seems to get tired
* Everyone likes him
* He'd never two-time you
* He's strong and independent
* He really seems to understand you

**He's a zero . . .** because he thinks it's cool to make jokes at other people's expense. He can be honest to the point of tactlessness and although he thinks his bizarre brand of humour is hilarious, very few people would agree. Plus . . .

* He can be cold and unfeeling sometimes
* He's a tad full of himself
* You never know where he is
* It's hard to know where he's going, where he's been or where he's coming from
* He's 100 per cent bonkers!

## Personality Alert!

You may love him cracking jokes, but you'll soon go off it when you realize that he just won't stop!

**He looks great . . .** because, although he's not traditionally good-looking, he has an interesting and unusual face with wide-apart eyes, prominent cheekbones, a wide smiley mouth and a cute nose. When it comes to clothes, he has a rather distinctive style all of his own.

**He's a state . . .** *because* he's got a rather distinctive style all of his own!

**Meet him . . .**
- at the gym. (He likes to keep his lithe physique in peak condition – just in case he's called upon to save the world or something . . . )
- at the cinema, checking out the latest arty, subtitled film.
- collecting for charity. (So don't worry about going out looking for him – he'll be on your doorstep, rattling a collection box at you, before you know it!)

**Impress him by . . .** being cool and independent. The less girlie you are, the better. Mind you, he's a sucker for a bit of recognition so, when you first meet him, tell him you remember his fantastic performance in the Year 8 school play, and he'll be all yours! He has an intense dislike of soppy, overly romantic females, so forget the elaborately wrapped chocs and buy him a chip butty instead!

**If you can't be bothered to do the running . . .** he can run fast enough for you both. To get your attention, he'll do impressions, tickle you with his wit and "wisdom" and make a million silly faces. He'll also play practical jokes on you and rib you mercilessly. He'll ask loads of personal questions but won't tell you much in return. If you like a laugh-a-minute man of mystery, then Mr Aquarius is sure to win your heart!

**Keep him by** . . . not questioning his movements; tolerating his strange little "quirks"; putting up with his rowdy mates; never getting hysterical; not gossiping; smiling constantly.

**Dump him when** . . . he insists on making you the butt of all his awful jokes.

**Love match:** Gemini, Leo and Libra lasses just can't say no to him.

**Top Aquarian totty:** Robbie Williams.

# Pisces (February 19–March 19)

**He's a hero** . . . because he's caring, helpful and, even as a mate, he'll always be there when you need him. As a boyfriend, he's really romantic, but that doesn't stop him from being a bit of a crazy party animal. Also . . .
* He's really loving

* He knows how to have a good time
* He's deep and philosophical
* He's always making romantic gestures
* He'll take you to fantasy-land (if you fancy it)
* He'd do anything for you

**He's a zero . . .** because his self-esteem is so low, it can be a drag always having to pump up his ego for him. Also, when it comes to practical stuff, he's just useless! (Q: How many Pisceans does it take to change a light bulb? A: Ten – nine to form a search party to go looking for a handyman and one to write a poem about it!) Plus . . .

* He's too scatty
* He doesn't know which way up he is
* He allows others to take advantage of him
* He's impressed by the dodgiest people
* He can't make a decision to save his life!

## Personality Alert!

He's a dithering dreamer and you could get fed up constantly trying to pull his dappy little head out of the clouds.

**He looks great . . .** in second-hand clothes. He's got a really sweet face with large, watery-looking eyes, dimples, a long nose and a pouty mouth. His hair is baby-soft and tends to have a public schoolboy floppiness about it. He's got excellent posture (you'll never see a Piscean guy slouching), is naturally graceful (get him up on a catwalk!) and is a lovely little mover (see him go on that dance floor!). He likes comfy clothes in unusual styles and natural fabrics.

**He's a state . . .** when he tries to look smart: it's just not him!

**Meet him . . .**
- at a jumble sale or charity shop. (He may even work there.)
- at the local swimming baths or aquarium. (Pisces *is* the sign of the fish.)
- at a publishing house, trying to get them to publish his poems.

**Impress him by . . .** buying or making him a present and posting it to him. Once he gets the message that you fancy him, he'll ask you out. (So make sure he knows it's from you . . . ) Once you get chatting to him, try not to be too argumentative – he hates confrontation; flatter him at every opportunity (telling him you dreamt about him is always a good chat-up line); and show him what a good listener you are. He loves that in a girl!

**If you can't be bothered to do the running . . .** he'll pursue you to the max. First, he'll try to impress you with his fancy footwork at the disco. If that doesn't work, he'll write you a song (and sing it to you too if you're "lucky"), send you flowers, and/or inundate you with love letters and other tokens of his affection. And he won't give up until you've at least acknowledged him (and his talents!)

**Keep him by ...** analysing his dreams for him; kissing him a lot; having younger siblings or cousins (Piscean blokes love kids); remembering all your silly little anniversaries; not laughing when he sings to you; keeping a straight face when he talks about how you and he were together in a past life.

**Dump him when ...** his love letters start making you feel bilious.

**Love match:** He's capable of loving forever – but only if you're a Cancerian, Virgoan or Scorpian girl.

**Top Piscean totty:** James Bradfield (Manic Street Preachers), Peter Andre, Jon Bon Jovi, Ronan Keating and Stephen Gately (Boyzone), Evan Dando and Graham Coxon (Blur).

# Love Match

*Check our specially devised compatibility chart over the page and discover whether or not you and the boy of your dreams are destined to be celestial soul-mates ...*

# LOVE MATCH COMPATIBILITY CHART

| IF HE'S ▶<br><br>AND YOU'RE ▼ | ARIES | TAURUS | GEMINI | CANCER | LEO |
|---|---|---|---|---|---|
| TAURUS | 🌸 | 🚲 | ⚽ | 🥤 | 🌸 |
| GEMINI | 🕶 | 🏈 | 🎈 | 🎩 | 🕶 |
| CANCER | ⛺ | 🍷 | 🎵 | 🎁 | ⛺ |
| LEO | 💘 | 🤝 | ☕ | 🐱🐶 | 💘 |
| VIRGO | 🌸 | 🚲 | ⚽ | 🥤 | 🌸 |
| LIBRA | 🕶 | 🏈 | 🎈 | 🎩 | 🕶 |
| SCORPIO | ⛺ | 🍷 | 🎵 | 🎁 | ⛺ |
| SAGITTARIUS | 💘 | 🤝 | ☕ | 🐱🐶 | 💘 |
| CAPRICORN | 🌸 | 🚲 | ⚽ | 🥤 | 🌸 |
| AQUARIUS | 🕶 | 🏈 | 🎈 | 🎩 | 🕶 |
| PISCES | ⛺ | 🍷 | 🎵 | 🎁 | ⛺ |
| ARIES | 💘 | 🤝 | ☕ | 🐱🐶 | 💘 |

First find your own compatibility symbo

| VIRGO | LIBRA | SCORPIO | SAGITTARIUS | CAPRICORN | AQUARIUS | PISCES |
| --- | --- | --- | --- | --- | --- | --- |

hen discover what it says about you and your star boy . . .

# Making It Work

*This system revolves around the elements. First find out which element you are by checking out your own symbol on the compatibility chart.*

If the symbols for your sign are – ⚔ 🔭 ☀ or 🐾 – you're **Miss Fire**, which means you:
- Are passionate, flirtatious and excitable
- Love a challenge
- Are outgoing and confident in most situations
- Can be nasty
- Would rather snog than talk!
- Find it hard to say "no"
- Are adventurous, daring and would try anything once
- Never hold back your emotions
- Don't take life too seriously

If the symbols for your sign are – 🌿 🚲 ⚽ or 🌽 – you're **Miss Earth**, which means you:
- Are sexy but subtle
- Are sensual, sensitive and very touchy-feely
- Are down-to-earth, hard-working, practical and reliable
- Have a great sense of humour
- Love all the good things in life
- Can be bossy

- Hate anyone saying "no" to you
- Could never be unfaithful
- Take love and life pretty seriously

If the symbols for your sign are – ✿ ● ❀ or ☕ – you're
**Miss Air**, which means you:
- Love a good gossip
- Can be a bit cool
- Have the ability to see people as they really are
- Are always on the phone
- Are childlike and uninhibited.
- Have trouble being faithful in a relationship
- Tend to speak your mind
- Love the thrill of the romantic chase
- Like to be logical, rational and controlled (even
  when some emotion is called for)

If the symbols for your sign are – ▲ ♏ ♫ or ♒ –
you're **Miss Water**, which means you:
- Are incredibly romantic
- Are sensitive to the needs, moods and feelings of
  others
- Need a lot of love, attention and affection
- Can be moody
- Have a fantastic imagination
- Don't mind someone else taking the lead in most
  situations
- Like art and literature
- Can be talked into doing things you'd rather not do
  at all
- Are a bit secretive

*Now you know which element you are, discover what you can do to make the relationship between you and your chosen bloke a success. Check the symbol for you and your star boy on the compatibility chart, and read on . . .*

What a red-hot combination this is! As two fiery Fire signs, this relationship is wild. The main trouble is though that as you're both so lusty, there's no way either of you can contain your desire for passing fancies and are unlikely to be able to stay the course. If either of you decide that you want to get serious, this fiery coupling will burn itself out fairly sharpish. Even if you stay together for the passion, it's unlikely to go on for ever: no one (not even someone as passionate as you) can stand *that* much heat!

*Make it work by . . .*
. . . At least *trying* to stay faithful
. . . Slowing down and realizing that love isn't a race or a competition
. . . Showing your soft side now and again – and that applies to both of you

As a Fire sign, you're a pretty realistic person and although you're enthusiastic when it comes to love, you don't have too many expectations about this romance. This Earth bloke has both feet firmly planted on the ground and, although you can be steady when you want to be, you may not want to be with *this* bloke, who may prove to be a bit of a drag in the long term. While you're lively and impulsive, he's sedate and cautious and sure to put a damper on any of your bright spark ideas. If you do end up together, then it has a reasonable chance of succeeding, but only if you can keep things interesting.

*Make it work by . . .*
. . . Making more of an effort to appreciate his sensible side (instead of ridiculing it)
. . . Telling him not to expect you to do all the work – especially when it comes to keeping the relationship alive
. . . Not forcing him to talk when he doesn't want to

His Airy personality may fan your Fire-y one, and although he may have a calming effect on you on one level, it may not make for much excitement. When you first meet, you're likely to be bowled over by his flirtatious charm, and a romance could flare up pretty quickly. He's a bit moody though, and the way he blows hot and cold is perhaps something you may not be able to handle. Generally, he allows you to take the lead and he's happy to do whatever you want, but your demands may prove too much for him in the end.

*Make it work by . . .*

. . . Being less demanding

. . . Not getting wound up by the things he says and does

. . . Remembering his needs as well as your own

You're Fire; he's Water. You're hot; he's cool. This doesn't mean he's not passionate – he is, but in a very gentle, romantic way. He's fairly traditional by nature and you shock him with your rather forceful personality. And whereas you like romance to be a bit of a laugh, he's deadly serious about it. If you're keen to make a go of this relationship, you may have trouble keeping the fires of passion burning past a certain point. But he's adaptable and willing to learn. And who better to teach him than you?

*Make it work by . . .*

. . . Appreciating and accepting your differences

. . . Taking him in hand

. . . Helping him look on the bright side of life

If you two get together – and you will because, although you're different in so many ways (you're an Earth sign and he's Fire), you share some basic qualities and interests – what may concern you most is his apparent lack of concern for you. You may look up to him at first, but as your relationship progresses, you realize that he may not be as romantic as you'd initially envisaged him to be. And because you like to be shown a lot of tenderness, this could bother you and could even put you off him. If you can give him the space and inspiration he requires, the flames of passion between you are capable of reaching great heights.

*Make it work by . . .*
. . . Teaching him how to be more caring
. . . Not placing him on a pedestal
. . . Giving him room to breathe within the relationship

What many might envisage to be a rather safe, possibly unexciting relationship, could easily become a rewarding and emotionally satisfying partnership. You're both Earth signs – gritty, practical and easy to read – and will have an instant liking for each other as soon as you meet. Together, you make a great team, warm and affectionate, each able to help the other free themselves from any insecurities. Because of this, your partnership should succeed.

*Make it work by . . .*
. . . Not letting others put you off each other
. . . Giving each other almost constant support and encouragement

... Not allowing jealousy or possessiveness to come between you

When you first set eyes on him, he's like a breath of fresh air (and he would be – he's an Air sign). You're a solid Earth sign and, to him, represent a port in the storm of life . . . at the start anyway. Although he's charming and extremely sociable, his weird moods may bother you intensely, especially when one minute he's incredibly immature, and the next he's a man of the world. When it comes to love, you know what you like but your lack of spontaneity may bore him. Not that you're boring – far from it – but he needs such constant variety that only a girl with the most powerful imagination and energy could really make him hers. But if you're willing to work at it, it might just turn out OK.

*Make it work by ...*
... Not expecting the relationship to work without either of you putting in any effort
... Being honest about what it is that bugs you both about each other
... Dealing with problems as and when they crop up

He needs a girl who's prepared to give him her all, and you may not be ready for all he's asking of you. You're

a realistic Earth sign and alarm bells start ringing for you even on your first date, when all he talks about is love and commitment. You may allow this to wash right over you (he *is* a mega-romantic Water sign, after all), and you find it hard to take such premature romantic rantings seriously. Romantically, he seems so experienced and this is what could make you fall for him. If he starts to believe his somewhat previous words of love, then he could easily fall for you too. This is a relationship that improves with age, so it may well be worth working at.

*Make it work by . . .*
. . . Making your feelings known at all times
. . . Not throwing it all in at the first sign of trouble
. . . Remembering that he's just as sensitive as you are

You're a beautiful Airy-fairy and it's hardly surprising that he's initially attracted by your looks. Once he gets to know you, he'll appreciate your wicked sense of humour. He's mesmerized by your ever-changing needs and unpredictable nature, and although this may irritate the hell out of a less challenge-seeking guy, he finds everything about you quite charming. He's a mega-direct Fire sign and you like the way he says what he thinks. You also love his obvious delight in you and his fun-loving, impulsive character. Together, you're constantly changing and, although this could destroy many a relationship, yours will positively thrive on it.

*Make it work by . . .*
. . . Keeping him entertained
. . . Putting a stop to his constant demands
. . . Not worrying about what other people think

As an Air sign, your head's stuck in the clouds when it comes to love; as an Earth sign, his feet are firmly on the ground. You may not think this pairing could work, but it might . . . mainly because he could just provide you with the stability and security you need (and secretly crave). Having said that, it's unlikely that you fancy him immediately and he may have to prove himself before you'll give him the time of day. He's impressed by your sociable personality (slightly envious too, if the truth be known) and is so proud of you. It's only when you start to feel constrained by his emotional needs and believe your individuality is threatened that you start to panic. This relationship can only work if you make an extra-special effort.

*Make it work by . . .*
. . . Being more realistic about your relationship
. . . Not expecting so much all the time
. . . Maintaining your independence

Air signs love a chat and when you two Airy types get

together, there's a whole lot of yakking going on! In fact, you talk so much, it's surprising if there's any time left for anything else! You realize pretty quickly how alike you are mentally, and because of this, you may be reluctant to spoil things by getting romantically embroiled. For those who *do* get involved, however, there are surprises that are well worth waiting for. Variety is the spice of your love life and you're both happy to go out of your way to work out new ways of having fun. A good pairing all in all.

*Make it work by . . .*
. . . Talking less and doing more
. . . Not being scared to admit your feelings for each other
. . . Keeping your romance exciting

You're attracted by his quiet, almost mysterious aura and he's charmed by your easy-going and friendly ways. You both possess a great sense of fun (you especially as a cheeky Air sign) and this is what brings you together ultimately. You're likely to have a great time too, although his regular bouts of insecurity and the fact that you never seem to want to do anything at the same time can bug you at times. His emotions run deep (and they would – he's a Water sign), but in the long term might cause far too many ripples in the relationship for your liking.

*Make it work by . . .*
. . . Making him feel secure (and that means no more
flirting with other boys!)
. . . Getting your body clocks in sync
. . . Not taking responsibility for his happiness

He's a Fire sign and you're attracted to his warm glow,
but no matter how hard you try to make him warm to
you, you'll soon have him raging. Because you're so
different from him, he sees you as a challenge and will
do his utmost to ruffle your cool surface. With regards
to love and romance, you're quite different, with him
being far more passionate than you. If you're one of the
more feisty Water signs, you may feel you've met your
match, but don't think for a second that you've got any
hold over him: he's his own person and if you try to pin
him down, the whole thing could get out of control,
ending in you getting seriously burnt.

*Make it work by . . .*
. . . Stopping winding each other up on purpose
. . . Being a bit more laid-back
. . . Looking on the bright side a bit more often

Although you're a Water sign and he's Earth, you're

similar in many ways and are naturally attracted to each other. You may be disappointed to find though, as time goes on, that he can be a bit of a tiresome stick-in-the-mud who doesn't appreciate your impetuous side. Nevertheless, he can provide you with comfort, stability and security; and you can help him to grow in every direction. If you can put up with the way he allows everyday life to interfere with your relationship, and if he can understand that you're not quite as practical as he is, then this relationship might be worth following through.

*Make it work by . . .*
. . . Understanding that you'll never really see eye to eye on certain matters
. . . Appreciating his bad points
. . . Letting him know when you're upset

His charm captivates you, but you can't understand why he finds it so hard to have eyes only for you. As a restless Air sign, he wants constant variety, and this may be a whim you're disinclined to entertain. In your opinion, he's a bit mad and, although you may find this exciting at first, you'll soon be wondering when he's going to start behaving "normally". Chances are, he won't. And when he realizes that as a commitment-keen Water sign you're after more than just a good time, he might fly off.

*Make it work by . . .*
. . . Not trying to change him
. . . Chilling out a bit
. . . Not swamping him with emotional demands

As two Water signs, your thoughts and feelings flow together naturally, and in theory you should get on fine. You both like to take the lead in love, but because you're both so sensitive, problems could arise. You're also both very possessive – him more so – and jealousy could cause many rows. On the up side, he can make you feel desirable and he feels you really understand him; if you want to make a go of it, you could form a very deep bond. But it won't be easy, that's for certain . . .

*Make it work by . . .*
. . . Taking it in turns to be boss
. . . Talking through any worries you have about your relationship
. . . Really *wanting* it to work

# The Venus Effect

*Discover where love planet Venus was on the day you were born and your romantic personality will be revealed . . .*

Look to the list below to find out which sign Venus was in on your birth day . . .

| <u>*Birth date*</u> | <u>*Venus was in . . .*</u> |
|---|---|
| **1979** | |
| Jan 1–6 | Scorpio |
| Jan 7–Feb 4 | Sagittarius |
| Feb 5–Mar 3 | Capricorn |
| Mar 4–28 | Aquarius |
| Mar 29–Apr 22 | Pisces |
| Apr 23–May 17 | Aries |
| May 18–Jun 11 | Taurus |
| Jun 12–Jul 5 | Gemini |
| Jul 6–31 | Cancer |
| Aug 1–23 | Leo |
| Aug 24–Sep 16 | Virgo |
| Sep 17–Oct 10 | Libra |
| Oct 11–Nov 3 | Scorpio |
| Nov 4–28 | Sagittarius |
| Nov 29–Dec 22 | Capricorn |
| Dec 23–31 | Aquarius |

### Birth date

### Venus was in . . .

**1980**

| | |
|---|---|
| Jan 1–15 | Aquarius |
| Jan 16–Feb 9 | Pisces |
| Feb 10–Mar 6 | Aries |
| Mar 7–Apr 3 | Taurus |
| Apr 4–May 12 | Gemini |
| May 13–Jun 4 | Cancer |
| Jun 5–Aug 6 | Gemini |
| Aug 7–Sep 7 | Cancer |
| Sep 8–Oct 4 | Leo |
| Oct 5–29 | Virgo |
| Oct 30–Nov 23 | Libra |
| Nov 24–Dec 17 | Scorpio |
| Dec 18–31 | Sagittarius |

**1981**

| | |
|---|---|
| Jan 1–10 | Sagittarius |
| Jan 11–Feb 3 | Capricorn |
| Feb 4–27 | Aquarius |
| Feb 28–Mar 23 | Pisces |
| Mar 24–Apr 17 | Aries |
| Apr 18–May 11 | Taurus |
| May 12–Jun 4 | Gemini |
| Jun 5–29 | Cancer |
| Jun 30–Jul 24 | Leo |
| Jul 25–Aug 18 | Virgo |
| Aug 19–Sep 12 | Libra |
| Sep 13–Oct 8 | Scorpio |
| Oct 9–Nov 5 | Sagittarius |
| Nov 6–Dec 8 | Capricorn |
| Dec 9–31 | Aquarius |

## _Birth date_                     _Venus was in . . ._

**1982**

| | |
|---|---|
| Jan 1–22 | Aquarius |
| Jan 23–Mar 1 | Capricorn |
| Mar 2–Apr 6 | Aquarius |
| Apr 7–May 4 | Pisces |
| May 5–30 | Aries |
| May 31–Jun 25 | Taurus |
| Jun 26–Jul 20 | Gemini |
| Jul 21–Aug 13 | Cancer |
| Aug 14–Sep 7 | Leo |
| Sep 8–Oct 1 | Virgo |
| Oct 2–25 | Libra |
| Oct 26–Nov 18 | Scorpio |
| Nov 19–Dec 12 | Sagittarius |
| Dec 13–31 | Capricorn |

**1983**

| | |
|---|---|
| Jan 1–5 | Capricorn |
| Jan 6–29 | Aquarius |
| Jan 30–Feb 22 | Pisces |
| Feb 23–Mar 18 | Aries |
| Mar 19–Apr 12 | Taurus |
| Apr 13–May 8 | Gemini |
| May 9–Jun 5 | Cancer |
| Jun 6–Jul 9 | Leo |
| Jul 10–Aug 26 | Virgo |
| Aug 27–Oct 5 | Leo |
| Oct 6–Nov 8 | Virgo |
| Nov 9–Dec 6 | Libra |
| Dec 7–31 | Scorpio |

| **_Birth date_** | **_Venus was in . . ._** |
|---|---|
| **1984** | |
| Jan 1–25 | Sagittarius |
| Jan 26–Feb 18 | Capricorn |
| Feb 19–Mar 14 | Aquarius |
| Mar 15–Apr 7 | Pisces |
| Apr 8–May 1 | Aries |
| May 2–26 | Taurus |
| May 27–Jun 19 | Gemini |
| Jun 20–Jul 13 | Cancer |
| Jul 14–Aug 7 | Leo |
| Aug 8–31 | Virgo |
| Sep 1–25 | Libra |
| Sep 26–Oct 19 | Scorpio |
| Oct 20–Nov 13 | Sagittarius |
| Nov 14–Dec 8 | Capricorn |
| Dec 9–31 | Aquarius |
| **1985** | |
| Jan 1–3 | Aquarius |
| Jan 4–Feb 1 | Pisces |
| Feb 2–Jun 5 | Aries |
| Jun 6–Jul 5 | Taurus |
| Jul 6–Aug 1 | Gemini |
| Aug 2–28 | Cancer |
| Aug 29–Sep 21 | Leo |
| Sep 22–Oct 16 | Virgo |
| Oct 17–Nov 9 | Libra |
| Nov 10–Dec 3 | Scorpio |
| Dec 4–26 | Sagittarius |
| Dec 27–31 | Capricorn |

### *Birth date*　　　　　　　　　*Venus was in . . .*

**1986**

| Birth date | Venus was in . . . |
|---|---|
| Jan 1–19 | Capricorn |
| Jan 20–Feb 12 | Aquarius |
| Feb 13–Mar 8 | Pisces |
| Mar 9–Apr 1 | Aries |
| Apr 2–26 | Taurus |
| Apr 27–May 21 | Gemini |
| May 22–Jun 15 | Cancer |
| Jun 16–Jul 11 | Leo |
| Jul 12–Aug 7 | Virgo |
| Aug 8–Sep 6 | Libra |
| Sep 7–Dec 31 | Scorpio |

**1987**

| Birth date | Venus was in . . . |
|---|---|
| Jan 1–6 | Scorpio |
| Jan 7–Feb 4 | Sagittarius |
| Feb 5–Mar 2 | Capricorn |
| Mar 3–28 | Aquarius |
| Mar 29–Apr 22 | Pisces |
| Apr 23–May 16 | Aries |
| May 17–Jun 10 | Taurus |
| Jun 11–Jul 6 | Gemini |
| Jul 7–29 | Cancer |
| Jul 30–Aug 23 | Leo |
| Aug 24–Sep 16 | Virgo |
| Sep 17–Oct 10 | Libra |
| Oct 11–Nov 3 | Scorpio |
| Nov 4–27 | Sagittarius |
| Nov 28–Dec 21 | Capricorn |
| Dec 22–31 | Aquarius |

| **_Birth date_** | **_Venus was in . . ._** |
|---|---|

**1988**

| Jan 1–15 | Aquarius |
|---|---|
| Jan 16–Feb 9 | Pisces |
| Feb 10–Mar 5 | Aries |
| Mar 6–Apr 3 | Taurus |
| Apr 4–May 17 | Gemini |
| May 18–26 | Cancer |
| May 27–Aug 6 | Gemini |
| Aug 7–Sep 6 | Cancer |
| Sep 7–Oct 4 | Leo |
| Oct 5–29 | Virgo |
| Oct 30–Nov 23 | Libra |
| Nov 24–Dec 17 | Scorpio |
| Dec 18–31 | Sagittarius |

**1989**

| Jan 1–10 | Sagittarius |
|---|---|
| Jan 11–Feb 3 | Capricorn |
| Feb 4–27 | Aquarius |
| Feb 28–Mar 23 | Pisces |
| Mar 24–Apr 16 | Aries |
| Apr 17–May 10 | Taurus |
| May 11–Jun 4 | Gemini |
| Jun 5–28 | Cancer |
| Jun 29–Jul 23 | Leo |
| Jul 24–Aug 17 | Virgo |
| Aug 18–Sep 12 | Libra |
| Sep 13–Oct 8 | Scorpio |
| Oct 9–Nov 4 | Sagittarius |
| Nov 5–Dec 9 | Capricorn |
| Dec 10–31 | Aquarius |

## Venus In Aries

*Ups:*

- You have a warm, loving nature
- You're always attractive to the opposite sex
- You have no fear about telling a boy if you fancy him
- You bring a lot of laughter into any relationship

*Downs:*

- You sometimes start rows just for the sheer hell of it
- You're not too good at choosing boyfriends, often ending up with someone totally unsuitable
- You don't find it easy to express your feelings
- You can be selfish

## Venus In Taurus

*Ups:*

- Your love life is uncomplicated
- You're good-looking and charming
- You're affectionate and attentive
- You're sensual, considerate and faithful

*Downs:*

- Your tendency to be over-possessive and jealous can cause problems
- You can easily get into a romantic rut
- You have the potential to "waste" your love on someone quite undeserving
- You've got a fierce temper if you don't get what you want

## Venus In Gemini

*Ups:*

- Guys can't get enough of you!
- You're ace at flirting
- You're really exciting company
- When love wanes, you find it easy to bounce back

*Downs:*

- You're easily bored and can end a potentially great romance because of that
- Your need to have two or three relationships simultaneously can get you into trouble
- You need constant mental stimulation (and, sadly, not many boys can provide that)
- You don't take other people's feelings seriously enough

## Venus In Cancer

*Ups:*

- You're loyal, loving and lovable
- Your ever-changing moods make you very interesting company
- When you get the right sort of attention, you blossom into one of the sexiest girls around
- You always mean what you say – even though you don't always say what you mean . . .

*Downs:*

- You're a slave to your emotions
- You're a bit unrealistic about love
- You're too trusting at times

- You're so scared of being hurt, you'll avoid getting too close to anyone

## Venus In Leo
*Ups:*
- You always stand out from the crowd
- You enjoy the whole process of forming relationships and love being in love
- You're generous, faithful and warm-hearted.
- You have the ability to make a boyfriend feel really special

*Downs:*
- You're so keen to be in a relationship, you rather rush into things and make loads of romantic mistakes
- Your sense of judgment isn't all that it should be
- You suffer more than your fair share of heartache
- You need loads of attention and don't always get it

## Venus In Virgo
*Ups:*
- You are emotionally generous, always eager to please the one you love
- You're caring and thoughtful
- You're an exciting mixture of homely and sexy
- Because you're so intelligent and level-headed, you don't make too many mistakes on the love front

*Downs:*
- You can be inhibited
- You can be a bit of a mother hen with your boyfriend
- Your fussiness means you can go for long periods boyfriend-free
- You're all too easily put off by things that really don't matter

## Venus In Libra

*Ups:*
- You're fun-loving and attractive
- You're extremely popular with the opposite sex and have no trouble charming the ones you fancy into submission
- You're sympathetic and fair-minded
- You always stay great mates with your exes

*Downs:*
- Your fear of hurting anyone's feelings means that you're just a girl who can't say no – and this gets you into all sorts of tricky situations
- Your love life is likely to be complicated
- Quite often, you fall in love just because you're in that sort of mood – and who the object of your affections might be is almost irrelevant
- You'd rather be with *anyone* than be alone

## Venus In Scorpio

*Ups:*
- You can cope with any problems love throws at you

- You're passionate, intense and quite unforgettable
- When in love, you're incredibly loyal
- You're very sexy

*Downs:*
- You take love and life too seriously sometimes
- You often go for unavailable types
- Because of your obsessive tendencies, you run the risk of developing major, destination-nowhere crushes
- When a relationship ends, you can get nasty, particularly if you feel you've been wronged

# Venus In Sagittarius
*Ups:*
- With your fantastic sense of humour and free-thinking ways, you're attractive to many members of the opposite sex
- In a relationship, you will enthral your partner with your fun-loving ways
- You're caring, warm and affectionate
- You're enthusiastic, energetic and communicative

*Downs:*
- As a naturally friendly and frank person, your openness is often taken the wrong way
- You need tons of freedom – something only a few boyfriends will be able to give you
- Your unpredictable behaviour baffles many a potential boyfriend
- You see love as some sort of game – and this can cause problems

## Venus In Capricorn

*Ups:*

- You're persistent and always get your man, no matter how long it takes
- You have a talent for choosing great boyfriends
- You're faithful, loving and loyal
- Your great sense of humour makes you very attractive

*Downs:*

- You can be too cool sometimes, causing boys to see you as aloof and stand-offish
- You don't allow yourself to get deep enough into relationships to feel comfortable about expressing yourself
- Your great sense of logic often holds you back from getting involved in the first place
- Flirting doesn't come easy to you

## Venus In Aquarius

*Ups:*

- You're physically very attractive and unquestionably cool
- You are always surrounded by admirers – even though you may be completely oblivious to them
- You're never short of potential boyfriends
- When you find someone who shares your outlook and understands your need for independence, you're an interesting and loyal partner

**Downs:**

- You can't differentiate between friendship and love and sometimes go out with someone who would have been best kept as a friend
- You fall in love far too easily
- You often make the mistake of trying to "change" boyfriends and most of them don't take kindly to this
- You tend to like a boy for what he *could* be rather than for what he is

## Venus In Pisces

**Ups:**

- You're one of the most romantic signs of the zodiac
- You write the best love letters and have even been known to pen the odd love poem!
- You're attractive, compassionate and sensitive
- There's a queue of lads waiting to go out with you!

**Downs:**

- You have problems with jealousy, arising from your own insecurities
- You find it hard ending a relationship, even when you know it's not working
- You're waiting for Mr Perfect and don't seem to realize that he may not exist
- You make far too many sacrifices for boyfriends who don't deserve it

# Part 4:

# Friends And Rivals

# Are You A Great Mate?

You're not the most gregarious person in the world and, because you don't warm to many people, those who are classed as a mate are very lucky indeed. You're a slow mover when it comes to making friends and take a while before you feel really at ease with your mates. It's worth the effort though, because once you take a liking to someone, you're warm, loving and very kind. You're a gentle soul and never nag or complain about your friends. You're trustworthy too – if a mate tells you a secret it will go no further, no matter how many chocolatey bribes you're offered by those desperate to know the gossip. Because of this, you're often the friend that people turn to in times of stress or need. You know how to have a good time too and, although you're generally a quiet type, your friends can be sure of fun when they go out with you. On the down side, however, you can be jealous and possessive, expecting the same sort of loyalty from your friends as you give to them. If a mate stands you up, although you won't drop them, you're capable of getting quite sulky and resentful. Any disloyalty from a friend is regarded as a breach of confidence and trust. As one of the most loyal signs, once you've established a friendship with someone, you're mates forever and will never, ever let them down.

## You make friends because you're:

- Affectionate
- Reliable
- Strong
- Trustworthy
- A great listener
- Good fun (most of the time)

## You lose friends because you're:

- Possessive
- A bit dismissive of any form of weakness
- Tactless
- Snobby
- Lazy
- Not wildly adventurous

# Who's Your Friend?

**Y**ou like people who know how to have a good time and who encourage you to go out in search of one. You need friends who are as reliable as you are, happy to plan way in advance, and blessed with excellent taste (i.e. the same taste as yours!). You love a chat, but are just as happy to listen. You don't need to go out to have a laugh: a quiet night in with a big curry, a couple of vids and a close friend is your idea of social bliss. You like people who are strong, but that doesn't mean you can't be sympathetic to a friend in one of their moments of weakness: as long as they're strong most of the time, that's fine by you. The people you admire most may be powerful, successful or even rich: you enjoy looking up to your friends and like to share in their success. Your real friends will include a few Cancerians, a couple of Virgoans and a Pisces or two. Capricorns are your best bet, though.

# Your Best Mate . . .

### . . . is the type of person who would:

- Happily leave you be when you want to be left alone
- Join you on the sofa to watch *Casualty* instead of going out raving
- Always stick by you (even if they don't believe in your principles 100 per cent)
- Buy you really classy chocs for your birthday – on top of all the other extravagant gifts, of course!
- Not talk about you behind your back
- Never say you are boring (even when you are!)

# The Other Signs As Friends

You've read all about what makes a Taurean friend. But what about the other eleven signs? Here's a list of their good and bad qualities . . .

## Geminians . . .

### . . . make great mates because they're:

- Spontaneous
- Helpful
- Tons of fun
- Amusing

### . . . are dead-end friends because they're:

- Never on time
- Prone to fibbing
- Fickle
- Unpredictable

## Cancerians . . .

### . . . make great mates because they're:

- Kind
- Hospitable
- Sensitive
- Loyal

### . . . are dead-end friends because they're:

- Hypersensitive

- Prone to bearing grudges – for ages!
- Judgmental
- Clingy

# Leos . . .
## . . . make great mates because they're:
- Great fun
- Generous
- Proud of you
- Loving

## . . . are dead-end friends because they're:
- Easily upset
- Likely to ignore you for no apparent reason
- Hard to get to know properly
- A bit pig-headed

# Virgoans . . .
## . . . make great mates because they're:
- Fussy about who they're friends with. (If you're a Virgoan's mate, count yourself privileged!)
- Refined
- Considerate
- Keen to help in any way they can

## . . . are dead-end friends because they're:
- Hypercritical
- Terrible worriers
- A bit sarky sometimes
- Always right (or *think* they are anyway . . . )

## Librans . . .

### . . . make great mates because they're:

- Loving and lovable
- Honest
- Fair
- Gentle

### . . . are dead-end friends because they're:

- *Sooo* indecisive
- Occasionally jealous (especially of mates who are prettier than them)
- A bit grumpy sometimes
- Very sulky (especially if you neglect them for any period of time)

## Scorpians . . .

### . . . make great mates because they're:

- Absolutely hilarious
- Really generous
- Always make you feel welcome (even when you call round at the worst possible moment!)
- Will never gossip about you (no matter what juicy morsels you entrust them with!)

### . . . are dead-end friends because they're:

- Lazy about getting in touch
- Even lazier about answering the phone (especially if they've got an answerphone to do it for them)
- Able to read your mind
- Liable to turn nasty if you upset them

# Sagittarians . . .

## . . . make great mates because they're:

- Sociable
- Always willing to stick up for their mates (even if they don't really agree with them)
- Honest
- Open-minded

## . . . are dead-end friends because they're:

- *Too* honest sometimes (some would call it totally tactless)
- Prone to temper tantrums
- Occasionally violent and abusive – verbally and physically
- Unable to keep a secret

# Capricornians . . .

## . . . make great mates because they're:

- Happy to stick by their nearest and dearest through thick and thin
- Sincere
- Wildly generous when it comes to their mates' birthdays
- Ever so kind (when they want to be)

## . . . are dead-end friends because they're:

- Terrible judges of character
- Quite vicious if they're rejected in any way
- Unnecessarily suspicious of everyone and sometimes test their friends – just to see how loyal they are
- Users – or are capable of using a mate to get something (or someone) they want

## Aquarians . . .

### . . . make great mates because they're:

- Intelligent and interesting
- Happy to make a lot of effort when it comes to staying in touch with friends
- Not bothered about being woken up at four in the morning to help a friend in need (most of the time anyway . . .)
- Majorly friendly and sociable

### . . . are dead-end friends because they're:

- Inclined to want everyone – mates especially – to live by their own rather high standards
- Always stealing your ideas
- Desperate to be the boss in all relationships
- Occasionally self-centred, in that sometimes they believe their problems are more important than anyone else's

## Pisceans . . .

### . . . make great mates because they're:

- Unbiased and unprejudiced
- Always willing to listen
- A real laugh
- Happy to do all the organizing when it comes to nights out (even though they're not very good at it. Aw, shame . . .)

### . . . are dead-end friends because they're:

- A bit disorganized and forgetful
- Very insecure
- Occasionally cold and offhand for no real reason
- Mad as snakes!

## Ariens . . .

. . . make great mates because they're:

- Warm
- Broad-minded
- Generous
- Entertaining

. . . are dead-end friends because they're:

- Selfish
- Often inconsiderate
- Competitive
- Impatient

# Forever Friends?

*Now you've got the general idea of what all the separate signs are like, check the friendship chart over the page to find out more about friendship compatibility . . .*

There's an astrological theory about friendship which revolves around the order of the signs. To discover how it works, take a look at the chart on the next page, find your sign down the side and your friends' signs along the top, make a note of the symbol/number where the two signs meet, then check the "key" panel below. This should give you a good indication of how you and your mates get on . . .

Friends And Rivals
..........................

# Friendship Chart

| Your friend's sign ▶ Your sign ▼ | Aries | Taurus | Gemini | Cancer | Leo | Virgo | Libra | Scorpio | Sagittarius | Capricorn | Aquarius | Pisces |
|---|---|---|---|---|---|---|---|---|---|---|---|---|
| Taurus | ✸ | ◎ | ※ | ✿ | ⊞ | ❀ | ❁ | ◉ | ⊕ | ❋ | ⊠ | ◔ |
| Gemini | ◔ | ✸ | ◎ | ※ | ✿ | ⊞ | ❋ | ❁ | ◉ | ⊕ | ❋ | ⊠ |
| Cancer | ⊠ | ◔ | ✸ | ◎ | ※ | ✿ | ⊞ | ❋ | ❁ | ◉ | ⊕ | ❋ |
| Leo | ❋ | ⊠ | ◔ | ✸ | ◎ | ※ | ✿ | ⊞ | ❋ | ❁ | ◉ | ⊕ |
| Virgo | ⊕ | ❋ | ⊠ | ◔ | ✸ | ◎ | ※ | ✿ | ⊞ | ❋ | ❁ | ◉ |
| Libra | ◉ | ⊕ | ❋ | ⊠ | ◔ | ✸ | ◎ | ※ | ✿ | ⊞ | ❋ | ❁ |
| Scorpio | ❁ | ◉ | ⊕ | ❋ | ⊠ | ◔ | ✸ | ◎ | ※ | ✿ | ⊞ | ❋ |
| Sagittarius | ❋ | ❁ | ◉ | ⊕ | ❋ | ⊠ | ◔ | ✸ | ◎ | ※ | ✿ | ⊞ |
| Capricorn | ⊞ | ❋ | ❁ | ◉ | ⊕ | ❋ | ⊠ | ◔ | ✸ | ◎ | ※ | ✿ |
| Aquarius | ✿ | ⊞ | ❋ | ❁ | ◉ | ⊕ | ❋ | ⊠ | ◔ | ✸ | ◎ | ※ |
| Pisces | ※ | ✿ | ⊞ | ❋ | ❁ | ◉ | ⊕ | ❋ | ⊠ | ◔ | ✸ | ◎ |
| Aries | ◎ | ※ | ✿ | ⊞ | ❋ | ❁ | ◉ | ⊕ | ❋ | ⊠ | ◔ | ✸ |

122

## Key:

◎ – If you and a friend are the same sign – Taurus in this instance – you're too similar. You can be friends, but because you're so aware of each other's failings, you're likely to drive each other mad and need to be extra tolerant.

❋ – If you make friends with a person who is one sign ahead of you – as a Taurus, this would be a Geminian – they're very different from you, but are in possession of many of the qualities that you aspire to have. This person is a real example to you, is able to teach you many things (if you're prepared to learn, that is), and can lead you from where you are now in life to the next stage. But, because of your obvious differences, you're unlikely to be best mates.

❋ – A friend whose sign is the one before yours – Aries in your case – may appear to be radically different from you on the surface, but has a great understanding of your innermost fears and desires. They're a good person to fall back on in times of trouble, as they can listen without being judgmental. But, if you go out socializing together, you're unlikely to have that great a time. (That's if you can even agree on where you are going to go and what you are going to do in the first place!)

◉ – Someone two signs ahead of you – and for you, as a Taurus, this would be a Cancer – is a person you're really comfortable with. This person is almost like a brother or sister to you: you're able to spend a lot of time in their company (in fact, many friends two signs apart can even live together quite happily), but this relationship won't be as exciting as others you might have. This mate is mega-loyal though, will always be there for you, so is well worth hanging on to.

✿ – A friend whose sign is two signs behind yours – a Pisces in your case – is capable of being a great mate. You may not have an overwhelming need to see a lot of each other, but when you do you're sure to have a fine time. It's unlikely that you'll ever get *really* close to this person, but stick with them and they'll prove what a good friend they can be time and time again.

⚃ – If your friend is three signs ahead of you – and as a Taurus, that would make them a Leo – you could find them rather difficult. Not difficult enough to put you off wanting to spend time with them, but more of a challenge. You have differing views on almost everything, but this just makes for plenty of heated debate. Occasionally, this person really gets on your nerves, but for the most part you find them *kind* of entertaining.

▦ – If you have a friend whose sign is three signs behind yours – a mate who's an Aquarius in your case, Miss Taurus – you may not be on the most intimate terms, but they often feel obliged to help you. You don't have an emotional or spiritual link with this person, but may see eye to eye on other matters – work, maybe; money, perhaps. They're the sort of friend you can rely on for sensible advice and are able to point you in the right direction on a practical level. But they have to be in the right frame of mind to do it . . .

� – If you've befriended an individual who is four signs ahead of you **or** four signs behind you – a Virgo or a Capricorn in your case – you share the same element (Earth, in this case) and are likely to have tons in common. Sometimes, you can feel envious of them, especially the friend who is four signs ahead of you (Virgo) and you may long to be as talented as they are. On the other hand, they can be a real inspiration to you, firing your ambitions and giving you lots of ideas, but if you spend too much time together, the envy could get the better of you in the end . . .

⊕ – A friend who's five signs ahead of you – and for you, Taurus, that would be a Libra – is *capable* of helping you get to where you want to be, but may not *want* to help you. Not much of a mate at all really . . .

✿ – Someone five signs behind you – a Sagittarius in your case – is so very alien to you, but there's something about them that you find interesting. It's not that you have anything in common with this person – you're like chalk and cheese – but you have a strange kind of respect for the way they run their life. Even though you don't understand much of their behaviour, for some reason you just can't help being mesmerized by them. Weird, or what?

◉ – Your opposite sign or the sign that's six signs

ahead of or behind your own – Scorpio in your case, Taurus – will be naturally attracted to you and, to start with, you may believe that you have a lot in common. On the surface it seems that way, but once you get to know each other you realize just how different you are. This can lead to conflict but, more often than not, it makes for an exciting (though unpredictable) friendship. You are different on every level – physical, intellectual and emotional – and, while this can be a pain sometimes, ultimately you seem to complement each other and get on just fine.

# With Friends Like That . . .

**Some signs of the zodiac really don't get on with other signs – not one little bit. Read on to discover who's who in the world of rivals . . .**

As a **Taurean**, you're a likeable sort, and no one would believe that you're capable of being nasty or disliking anyone. But, deep down, you're just as capable as anyone else of upsetting people and making enemies. The sign that bugs you the most is **Leo** – you just *can't* get on with them; and, although **Librans** are ruled by the same planet as Taurus (Venus), that's about all you've got in common. You're unlikely to receive hate mail from these people though – mainly because it's **Sagittarians** and **Aquarians** who are your worst enemies . . . They just don't understand you at all and that worries them enough to actively dislike you.

### And the other signs?

## Gemini

Geminians are friendly and give most people the benefit of the doubt. Everybody except virtuous **Virgoans** that is, who, although ruled by planet Mercury (the same planet that rules Gemini), are a right royal pain in the butt to slightly immoral Gemini! **Scorpio** folk aren't too popular with Geminians either: they're just *soooo* infuriating! (In Gemini's opinion anyway.) But any poison pen letters that land on a Geminian's doormat are most likely to have been sent by a **Capricornian** (who finds Gemini's ways immensely aggravating) or a **Piscean** (who could be just plain jealous).

## Cancer

Cancerians sometimes seem to hate everyone – they get *that* grumpy! The people they consistently dislike are **Librans** and **Sagittarians**. Librans are so blimmin' wishy-washy (in Cancer's opinion) and Sagittarians don't seem to have anything in common with Cancer at all. Which is strange, because Libra and Sagittarius don't have too many problems with Cancer. But it's **Aquarians** and **Ariens** who find Cancerians the most bugsome. Such is life, eh?

## Leo

Leos aren't overly keen on **Scorpians** (for a myriad of reasons) and **Capricornians** (who seem only to be friendly to Leo when they want something). In return though, Scorpio tries to lean on Leo on occasion and Capricorn kind of looks up to them, but that doesn't really interest Leo. Real rivals aren't these folk at all though: Leos should watch out for **Taureans** (such as yourself) and **Pisceans** – they're the ones out to get 'em! Yikes!

## Virgo

Virgoans are right old fusspots and, because they're so picky when it comes to mates, should sometimes count themselves lucky to have any mates at all! The people who peeve them the most are **Sagittarians** and **Aquarians**: Virgo has no use for them at all. But real enemies come in the form of **Ariens** and **Geminians** – they've *really* got it in for Virgo.

## Libra

Librans are real sweethearts but that doesn't stop them disliking people from time to time. They're generally patient types but can, on occasion, get irritated. Top offenders, in Libra's eyes, are **Capricornians** and **Pisceans** – they're such a pain! But if anyone's going to boil a Libran's bunny, it'll be a **Taurean** (yes, you!) or a **Cancerian**. They might *seem* soft, but when they get riled, they get *really* riled. (And sometimes all it takes is a Libran getting in their way.)

## Scorpio

Scorpios are sometimes a tad paranoid and need trustworthy types as mates; that's why a rowdy **Arien** or a blabbermouth **Aquarian** wouldn't do as a mate at all. It's a shame, because those two signs are really quite fond of Scorpio. In fact, Miss Scorpio would be seriously surprised to discover who'd be most likely to hide sardines in her curtain pole: it'd be none other than a crazy **Gemini** or a mad **Leo**. Who'd have thought it, eh?

## Sagittarius

Sagittarians like a laugh so wouldn't be seen dead with one of you stick-in-the-mud **Taureans** or a moochy old **Piscean** (Saggie's opinion only). A Sagittarian would be more inclined to seek out the company of a **Cancerian** or a **Virgoan**, which is a shame because *they'd* probably turn Saggie down, due to the fact that they find them really annoying . . . Sad but true.

## Capricorn

Capricornians need friends, but they will not tolerate **Ariens** or **Geminians** under any circumstances. Not that these signs would cause them any harm – as you know, Aries and Gemini types don't actually pay too much attention to Capricorns at all. The people Capricornians should steer well clear of – and who could, if they wanted to, do untold damage to a Capricorn's reputation – are **Leos** (who find Caps immensely dull) and **Librans** (who won't even spare them the time of day).

## Aquarius

Aquarians like excitement but, in their opinion, that's

not something they'll get from ploddy old **Taureans** (i.e. you!) and depressing old **Cancerians**. Not that these folk are particularly nasty to Aquarius. Oh no. Real enemies come in the guise of vicious (and they *can* be when the mood takes them) **Virgoans** and spiteful **Scorpians**: they're the ones who'll plant cress seeds in your carpet and water it while you're on holiday . . .

## Pisces

Pisceans like a laugh; so do **Leos**. The trouble is, neither sign is that funny (not in each other's opinion anyway), so laughs would be seriously lacking if they ever got together. Pisceans often find themselves *mildly* amused by **Geminians**, but once within twenty paces of each other, rubbing up the wrong way begins. But the people Pisceans should really make an effort to avoid are **Librans** and **Sagittarians** – they aren't normally nasty, but they just can't resist bullying a Piscean.

## Aries

Ariens may have a lot of mates but, if the truth be known, they don't actually like many people at all. Which is strange because, all in all, they're pretty popular themselves. The people they dislike most tend to be other **Ariens**, **Cancerians** and **Virgoans**. If they get hate mail, it *may* be from an Arien, but it's more likely to be sent by a **Scorpian** or **Capricornian**, who aren't overly keen on rams at all.

# Part 5:

# Home And Family

# Taurus At Home

*You're definitely a family-orientated person and enjoy the company of your nearest and dearest. So long as you have a happy, harmonious home, you're an easy person to live with. But if there are too many conflicts, there's a tendency for you to withdraw into yourself – and your room.*

## Your Room

As a sensuous, luxury-loving Taurus, your room must be spacious and comfy. A wall-to-wall carpet or thick rug will be a must, as will a solid bed, squishy duvet, pretty-looking bed linen, loads of cushions and, ideally, velvety curtains. It's vital you feel cosseted, snug and safe. You're a fairly conventional person when it comes to interior design so quirky, modern styles aren't really your thing. You may even still have the furniture you grew up with but you don't mind – it gives you a sense of permanence. Flowers and plants are important to you so you're likely to have some kind of arrangement in your room. Taureans love little knick-knacks and ornaments, which means your room may look a bit cluttered. You'll probably have some valuable stuff on display, too. You're a bit of a collector on the quiet, with an eye for quality. TV in the bedroom? Possibly. But you usually prefer listening to your favourite music so a sound system is a must. Being a hospitable soul, you probably won't mind sharing a room, but at heart you'd much rather have your own individual space which you can decorate in your own sumptuous way. You have no problems choosing colour schemes – green, pink and pale blue – the colours of Venus your ruling planet – tend to dominate.

# Happy Families?

F amily life is very important to you and a stable home gives you the security you crave. But maybe those you live with aren't so clear-cut about what they want.. and this could cause problems. The star signs of the individual family members have great bearing on how you get on. There's an astrological theory that if you're one of the "masculine" signs (i.e. Aries, Gemini, Leo, Libra, Sagittarius or Aquarius), you'll be most influenced throughout your childhood by your dad; and if your star sign is "feminine" (i.e. Taurus, Cancer, Virgo, Scorpio, Capricorn or Pisces), then you're more likely to be influenced by your mum. As a Taurus, you'll probably find that it's your mum who exerts the most power over you.

# You And Your Parents*

*Taurean kids are generally happy, friendly little souls but, boy, can you be stubborn! On the other hand, your parents are forever boasting about how little trouble you are!*

An **Arien** parent will probably drive you mad because they're always on at you for not being as get-up-and-go as they are. Things should improve if they're able to understand that you like to do things in your own time.

You'll be in family heaven with **Taurean** parents. Like you, they're warm, down-to-earth individuals who tend to enjoy life at a leisurely pace. Don't get *too* cosy though. Do you really want to be spending your Saturday nights with mum and dad for ever more?

If one or both of your parents is a **Gemini**, your family life probably isn't that easy. To you, they're irritating, and a bit . . . well . . . weird, constantly chattering and permanently entertaining guests. You just wish they were like everyone else's parents.

A **Cancer** mum will provide the loving, secure home you crave, while you should be able to confide in a sensitive **Cancer** dad. Trouble is, they can be a bit too emotional for your practical nature.

**Leo** is the traditional sign of fatherhood and if your dad's a liony type, you'll admire him 'cos he's just so enthusiastic about life. But Leo parents just love to

*If you don't live with your parents, consider the star signs of your guardian/s or main carer/s instead.

show off – about everything. And if you're not a rapt enough audience, you could be in for trouble.

You and a **Virgo** parent? They like an orderly kind of life, which suits you. They also always have time for you. Watch out though, a Virgo parent can be very critical.

Like you, **Libran** parents are ruled by Venus which means, like you, they enjoy the good things in life. They're easy-going kind of people – maybe *too* easy-going. There are times when a few more rules would be better for you.

**Scorpio** parent? You'll like the fact that they go by the book for most things but sometimes they're just so serious. And talk about pushy! Plus a Scorpio mum can be especially moody and emotional.

**Sagittarius** parents are pretty easy going. They're enthusiastic about everything, realize you're your own person and don't have ridiculously high expectations. But you've nothing in common. Sad but true.

You tend to respond well to **Capricorn** parents, but you could clash because Capricorns tend to be fairly thrifty people who don't necessarily approve of your love of luxury.

You could well clash with an **Aquarian** parent. The fact that that they have such a quirky outlook on life may really get on your nerves, while your stubbornness may frustrate them. Accept that you're very different though and you should get along OK.

**Piscean** mas and pas like to relive their own youthful ambitions in their kids. As Pisces is a bit of an arty sign, this may not go down too well with practical you. However, you'll love the fact that Pisces mum in particular will be unfailingly caring.

# Any Brothers
# Or Sisters?

*Smiley, happy Taureans make nice
brothers and sisters but that stubborn streak has the
potential to send siblings up the wall. Being a bit
possessive, the Taurean may also dislike having to
share mum and dad. As Taurus is quite obedient
with a tendency to play it safe, louder sisters and
brothers may try to dominate. Don't let them. It's
also important that you don't overprotect a much-
loved sibling. So which star sign suits you best as a
sister or brother?*

**A**ries **brother** or sis? Er, not the best combination.
Your **Arien brother** will be too feisty for your
liking while a sis will be so loud and bossy,
she'll probably drive you nuts.

A **Taurus sibling** will suit you fine. You'll like the
same things, and go at the same pace. However you're
both so stubborn, it'll be stalemate most of the time.

You'll be amused by your **Gemini brother** because
he'll really know what makes you laugh, but his
unreliable ways will make you blow a fuse. **Gemini
sister**? She'll make you laugh, too, but she's really too
flighty and flirty to be a soulmate.

**Cancer siblings** will bring out the mother in you. But
remember, don't smother! Cancerian moodiness may
well drive you mad but, on the whole, you get on OK.

You may well look up to an older **Leo sibling** (a

brother in particular), because they're just so dynamic. Their constant showing off could annoy you however, and little Leo sibs will bring out your stubborn streak.

A **Virgo sister** is likely to be a great mate since she's an Earth sign like you. You'll admire her for her brains while she'll value your practical good sense. **Virgo brother**? His faddiness may annoy you.

You'll get on with either your **Libra brother** or **sister**. Also ruled by Venus, like you they enjoy the good things in life and you probably spend hours discussing your most favourite ever nosh-up.

A **Scorpio sibling** is likely to be even more determined than you, which could lead to conflict; also frustration may arise on your part when they refuse to open up to you.

The pranks of your **Sagittarius brother** or **sister** will make you laugh, but you'll worry about them too. You'll get on when they're in a quiet mood, but when they're feeling crazy they just don't know when to stop.

You'll enjoy talking money with **Capricorn brothers** and **sisters** – they love the stuff even more than you do.

It's doubtful you'll really understand an **Aquarius sibling**. They're simply too idealistic for you. Older siblings, in particular, are likely to have wacky ideas.

Younger **Pisces siblings** may seem so vulnerable, you want to wrap them in cotton wool. Resist the temptation. You'll probably be an older Pisces brother or sister's greatest confidante – you're practical, they're emotional.

If you want to find out more about compatibility within your family, check out the chart opposite . . .

Are you compatible with your family? Check out this destiny chart and find out . . .

| Your Sign | Your perfect mum is . . . | Your perfect dad is . . . | Mum from hell is . . . | Dad from hell is . . . | Best brother is . . . | Best sister is . . . |
|---|---|---|---|---|---|---|
| TAURUS | Taurus or Virgo | Scorpio or Capricorn | Gemini | Sagittarius | Cancer | Gemini |
| GEMINI | Aries or Sagittarius | Gemini or Aquarius | Pisces | Taurus | Leo | Cancer |
| CANCER | Cancer or Libra | Pisces or Taurus | Sagittarius | Aquarius | Virgo | Leo |
| LEO | Aries or Cancer | Scorpio or Aquarius | Libra | Capricorn | Libra | Virgo |
| VIRGO | Cancer or Virgo | Capricorn or Taurus | Aries | Leo | Scorpio | Libra |
| LIBRA | Gemini or Libra | Aries or Aquarius | Scorpio | Cancer | Sagittarius | Scorpio |
| SCORPIO | Scorpio or Pisces | Taurus or Capricorn | Cancer | Gemini | Capricorn | Sagittarius |
| SAGITTARIUS | Gemini or Aquarius | Aries or Leo | Taurus | Scorpio | Aquarius | Capricorn |
| CAPRICORN | Taurus or Capricorn | Virgo or Scorpio | Aquarius | Libra | Pisces | Aquarius |
| AQUARIUS | Gemini or Leo | Libra or Scorpio | Capricorn | Virgo | Aries | Pisces |
| PISCES | Libra or Scorpio | Pisces or Cancer | Leo | Aries | Taurus | Aries |
| ARIES | Aries or Leo | Libra or Sagittarius | Virgo | Pisces | Gemini | Taurus |

# Your Future Family

*How many times you marry, the number of children you'll have and whether or not you'll have a happy family life in the future all depends on your Sun Sign (Taurus) combined with your Rising Sign. Check out your Rising Sign on pages 6–19, then check what it reveals below.*

## You're a Taurus with ...

**Aries Rising.** Impetuous – that's you! You may well marry young but live to regret it. However you'll either come through it or end up with someone else. You may have kids but it's not absolutely certain.

**Taurus Rising.** You're passionate but faithful, so once

married you're likely to stay that way. Family life is very important to you and your kids will bring you great satisfaction.

**Gemini Rising.** You old flirt, you! You'll have loads of flings before you meet the right man. When you do, he'll be a friend as well as a life partner. Your kids (you're likely to have two) will bring out your softer side.

**Cancer Rising.** You're in danger of settling down for money rather than love. You'll probably have kids, but may well become deeply attached to several other children as well.

**Leo Rising.** You're oh-so-loving and two marriages or long-term relationships are forecast, with children by both partners – possibly twins if one of your men is Aquarius.

**Virgo Rising.** You secretly like excitement so it's possible you'll have a fling or two once you're married (naughty!) Yes, you'll have children but certainly not a brood.

**Libra Rising.** Once you've made up your mind about marrying (which is likely to take ages), the lucky man may well be from a large family. Your own family won't be as big but you'll be happy.

**Scorpio Rising.** You have high standards. There's

nothing wrong with this, apart from the fact that it could create difficulties with your future family. You may have a couple of partners and loadsakids!

**Sagittarius Rising.** There's nothing you like more than a bit of passion and excitement, but you tend to be rather logical when it comes to love. Partner? One. Kids? Probably two.

**Capricorn Rising.** You like being independent, so it'll be a while before you decide to settle down. Once you do, the man in question will have a great influence on you. You'll be a good parent.

**Aquarius Rising.** You'll marry, probably quite early on in life, and it'll be a real forever thing. Your husband is likely to be some kind of artist. You'll have a couple of kids – they may even be twins!

**Pisces Rising.** You old romantic! You'll fall in love many times throughout your life, but still believe that marriage is for life. You'll probably marry late and you're destined to have at least two kids, who will bring you great fulfilment.

# Pet Power!

**And finally . . . pets. They're members of the family too, you know! Check the chart below and discover which animals are for you and which pets you prefer.**

| Your Sign | Favourite farm animal | Favourite wild animal | Perfect pet | You like a pet to be . . . |
|---|---|---|---|---|
| **Taurus** | Bull | Elephant | Dog | Reliable |
| **Gemini** | Collie dog | Tiger | Parrot | Responsive |
| **Cancer** | Pig | Dolphin | Rabbit | Lovable |
| **Leo** | Cockerel | Lion | Puppy | Fun |
| **Virgo** | Cow | Orang-utan | Budgie | Clean |
| **Libra** | Baby chick | Monkey | Cockatoo or dove | Pretty |
| **Scorpio** | Goose | Shark | Tarantula or snake | Scary! |
| **Sagittarius** | Horse | Zebra | Pony or horse | Sporty |
| **Capricorn** | Goat | Crocodile | Cat | Self-sufficient |
| **Aquarius** | Donkey | Kangaroo | Tree frog | Interesting |
| **Pisces** | Sheep | Whale | Goldfish | Dependent |
| **Aries** | Ram | Rhino | Rat or mouse | Fast-moving |

# Part 6:
# School, Career, Hobbies, Money

# Are You The Perfect Pupil?

*You're a trier that's for sure, but you're not exactly every teacher's dream. As a Taurus, you like to do things your own way – and that includes studying. No one – not even the most determined teacher – can make you do something if you don't want to: if you're cornered in this way, you'll go into a huge obstinate sulk and refuse to pay attention at all. You do need the occasional kick up the behind though: if left to your own devices, you can be incredibly lazy. Generally you work slowly but steadily in an orderly way, and it's worth it because you tend to get reasonable results.*

Although you're not overly keen on school, in the classroom you tend to be consistent. Your fave subjects are technical and scientific subjects (this includes cooking), but you may have trouble with the basic stuff – Maths, English and languages. You're actually quite an arty type and, although this may not be immediately obvious, you should be encouraged to develop these creative talents. If you don't understand something, and if you don't get the support and encouragement you need, you give up really easily. This can be very frustrating for teachers who can see your potential. More than anything, you need to be allowed to take your time over your work: if you're rushed, it can put you off.

In class, you like to keep a low profile and make an effort not to attract too much attention to yourself. Your classmates see you as fairly quiet. You don't go out of your way to make friends – you usually wait until you're approached. You're a follower rather than a leader, but tend not to hang out in large gangs anyway, being more of a one-on-one type. Taurean females usually have a couple of really close mates and that's enough for them.

If you want to see how your mates compare as schoolmates and pupils, refer to the chart on the opposite page . . .

Study this specially devised chart and work out what kind of student you are . . .

| Your Sign | As a student you're . . . | Your fave subject is . . . | Most compatible teacher is . . . | You'd get detention for . . . | Your perfect classmate is . . . |
|---|---|---|---|---|---|
| TAURUS | Slow but determined | Science | A Cancerian | Sulking | A Scorpian |
| GEMINI | Irritatingly clever | Languages | A Leo | Writing notes | A Sagittarian |
| CANCER | Quiet and studious | Cookery | A Virgoan | Eating sweets in class | A Capricornian |
| LEO | Attention-seeking | English language | A Libran | Messing about | An Aquarian |
| VIRGO | Chatty and hardworking | English literature | A Scorpian | Being cheeky | A Piscean |
| LIBRA | Lively and creative | Needlework | A Sagittarian | Rule-breaking | An Arien |
| SCORPIO | Serious and ambitious | History | A Capricornian | Being sarcastic | A Taurean |
| SAGITTARIUS | Nothing but trouble | Geography | An Aquarian | Not doing your homework | A Geminian |
| CAPRICORN | Teacher's pet! | Maths | A Piscean | Letting your work be copied | A Cancerian |
| AQUARIUS | A bit hard to handle | Social studies | An Arien | Skiving | A Leo |
| PISCES | Lazy but imaginative | Art | A Taurean | Not paying attention | A Virgoan |
| ARIES | Noisy but bright | PE | A Geminian | Shouting | A Libran |

# Just The Job

*Many Taureans become rich through their work. You want to land a job where you can get on with it without interference from others, so becoming self-employed might be an option. On the other hand, you'd like a career that draws admiration from your friends, so could go for something well-respected or even glamorous.*

Taureans are associated with money, agriculture, food and beauty and could end up in a job connected to these areas. Banking, stockbroking, farming, floristry or catering would be suitable. Working as a chef or beautician would also appeal. You're a good singer too and could – if you really wanted to – become a professional songstress.

Wherever you work your surroundings should be pleasant. If you work at a desk, it'll be neat and tidy. You hate noisy environments and will avoid a job where the decibel level is too high.

You're reliable and honest, and are always cool in an emergency: employer heaven! If you're the boss, you're fair and patient, but won't be messed about or taken advantage of.

# Hobbies

As a laid-back Taurean, you like hobbies that bring you a lot of pleasure with minimal exertion! If you do indulge in anything physical, it's likely to be bike riding, swimming or horse riding. The main Taurean hobby is singing. You also like collecting things of value and may find antiques interesting. Some Taureans enjoy a spot of gardening and the more arty ones may indulge in a bit of painting or drawing.

# Will You Be Rich?

**How likely you are to get rich can depend on your star sign.**

As a Taurus, you're very interested in making money (mainly because of the security it can bring). You won't fall for get-rich-quick schemes and could take a while building up your wealth. As you get older, you could get involved in stocks and shares as a

hobby. But remember that sometimes the best things in life are free. If you can understand this, you'll not only become mega-loaded in the future, but happy too!

## Astro-cash facts:

- The people most likely to get rich are (in this order) Leos, Taureans, Sagittarians and Virgoans. These signs are closely followed by Aries, Capricorn, Cancer, Scorpio, Libra, Gemini and Aquarius. The least likely sign to accumulate great wealth is Pisces (unless you're Cindy Crawford or Drew Barrymore, that is – both Pisceans and both rather loaded).

- Leos get richest the quickest. But they need to focus on making money and not be distracted by all the other stuff that life hurls their way.

- Cancerians are destined to get rich through their own efforts and shrewdness. They won't get rich, however, if they sit back and relax every time they have a minor success: they must keep on keeping on if they want to make it Branson-style.

- If you were born when Jupiter was in Taurus, great wealth will be yours. Jupiter was in Taurus from 12 April 1964 until 22 April 1965. It moved through the sign again from 26 March 1976 to 22 August 1976 and, again, from 17 October 1976 to 3 April 1977. It returned to Taurus on 9 March 1988 until 21 July 1988, and again from 1 December 1988 until 10 March 1989. Its most recent visit to the sign was on the 28 June 1999 where it stayed until 22 October 1999. The next time this transit occurs will be from 15 February 2000 until 29 June 2000. Anyone born during any of these periods is born to be rich!

# Part 7:
# Holidays

# Sun, Sand And Stars!

*Taureans, when they can be bothered with it, love a good holiday! If you want to find out which countries are a-calling, how to get there and who your top travelling companion should be, you've come to the right place . . .*

Taureans are homely types, who often can't be bothered with all the fuss and bother of going away on holiday. Given the choice, you'd rather stay in bed for a couple of weeks! When you do decide to go away, you like to have plenty of time to gather yourself. You need to know you'll have enough spending money, just as much as you like to know where you're going and what your destination has to offer in the way of facilities. Weather-wise, you're not overly keen on hot climates, because when you get hot you get sleepy. You love sampling local cuisine though, and you're happy to spend hours browsing around all the souvenir shops.

## Do What? (And Where?)

You like to spend your free time somewhere as much like home as possible – or at least somewhere where you know the food will be good and you'll have somewhere comfortable to sleep. And although you love to relax, this doesn't necessarily mean flopping around on a beach. Bring out the more artistic, less lazy side of your nature and try a holiday which involves actually doing something creative.

## How To Get There
Slowly. You like to take in the scenery, so flying may be too quick a method for you. You'll fly if you have to, but luxury trains and coaches are your favoured mode of transport. You're not keen on long journeys, so make sure you've got someone to talk to, a big window to look out of, or a favourite book to read.

## Holiday Horrors
You're so worried about not feeling comfortable, you're often put off doing anything adventurous. This can be a problem for anyone who might be holidaying with you . . . unless you're with another Taurean of course. Try to sacrifice comfort for experience sometimes – you might learn something!

## Best Holidays . . .
will be had in Ireland, Russia, the Greek Islands, Capri, Cyprus and Switzerland.

| Your Sign | What you need | Holiday love with ... | Activities | Travel ... | Holiday horrors |
|---|---|---|---|---|---|
| TAURUS | Time | a Scorpian | Relaxing | slowly | Being too lazy and missing out |
| GEMINI | Stimulation | a Sagittarian | Socializing and sightseeing | by plane | Stomach upsets |
| CANCER | Homely surroundings | a Capricornian | All types of watersports | by water | Stress |
| LEO | Sunshine | an Aquarian | Sunbathing | in style! | Sunburn! |
| VIRGO | Culture | a Piscean | Skiing and snowboarding | by train | Catching lurgies |
| LIBRA | New experiences | an Arien | Walking and cycling | first-class | Over-indulgence, in snogging especially! |
| SCORPIO | Mystery and excitement | a Taurean | Drawing and touring | Taxi! | Dehydration (in hot countries) |
| SAGITTARIUS | Thrills! | a Geminian | Riding and skateboarding | by motorbike | Being conned |
| CAPRICORN | Peace and quiet | a Cancerian | Camping | on foot | Getting bored |
| AQUARIUS | Freedom | a Leo | Safari and nature treks | any way | Running out of money |
| PISCES | Peace and quiet | a Virgoan | Fishing and picnicking | by boat | Being disappointed |
| ARIES | Lots of action | a Libran | Pony-trekking and swimming | fast! | Accidents |

# Part 8:
# Party On!

# Taurus – The Take It Or Leave It Party Girl

*What's your social style? Are you a party animal or a bit of a party pooper? Read on to find out whether you (and your mates) are the life 'n' soul . . .*

You love going out, but you like plenty of warning. Preparing yourself physically, mentally and spiritually for a big night out takes more than a few minutes for a girl like you. Sometimes you can be bit lazy and decide that partying's just not worth the effort, opting instead for a quiet night in with a big bowl of Doritos and a rented video. Your mates may get irritated by your take-it-or-leave-it party attitude and will sometimes get a bit fed up having to shoe-horn you out of your bean bag only to watch you sitting in the corner of the party all night, wearing a rather long face and wishing you were at home. Once

you're in the mood though (and the mood does take you BIG-time on occasion), you can rave as good as the rest. And you can stay up longer too. But that's Taurean stamina for you . . .

**Your perfect party:** A karaoke do in a nice restaurant (Taureans love a good croon), then home to bed  - not too late though (Taureans love a good kip too!)

**Craziest party stunt:** Falling asleep under the pile of coats in the spare room.

**Going out . . .** is a chore if you're not in the right mood; fine if you are.

**Staying in . . .** doesn't bother you: it suits your couch-potato personality!

# Your Partying Friends

*And what about your mates? Here's a quick run-down of the other eleven signs . . .*

## Gemini

All Geminians love their social lives to be varied and thrilling and if they're not, they'll get bored and grumpy. Not that they're asking to be entertained – Gems are more than happy to organize their own activities.

**Perfect party:** A top house party at a mate's house, where they can arrive early, get ready, and help with the proceedings.

**Craziest party stunt:** Copping off with every member of the opposite sex there – regardless of who they're going out with! (Tut tut!)

**Going out** . . . perks 'em up.

**Staying in** . . . gets 'em down.

# Cancer

It has to be said that Cancerians aren't exactly famous for their round-the-clock partying. At the risk of appearing boring, they prefer staying in – especially if there's any eating of delicious snacks to be done!

**Perfect party:** A dinner party – food cooked by the Cancerian – for a few close chums.

**Craziest party stunt:** Staying out past midnight.

**Going out . . .** is unavoidable sometimes.

**Staying in . . .** means lots of lovely quality time . . . with themselves. Luxury!

# Leo

Everyone knows how gorgeous and fun-loving Leos can be, but may *not* know what control freaks they are. Being someone else's guest can be unnerving for a Leo. On the other hand, they make totally fab hosts.

**Perfect party:** A party at home, with scrummy grub, plenty of dancing and Leo, as ever, in the spotlight.

**Craziest party stunt:** Going to someone else's party and actually enjoying it!

**Going out . . .** is fine if they know what to expect and can spend at least *most* of the evening being the centre of attention.

**Staying in . . .** is a reasonably enjoyable necessity.

# Virgo

Virgos aren't 100 per cent comfortable at a rowdy party. In a Virgoan's view, parties aren't so much social occasions, but are more a way of networking. Most Virgoans prefer spending time in their own company.

**Perfect party:** A sleep-over with a couple of their closest girl friends.

**Craziest party stunt:** Dancing.

**Going out . . .** gives others the pleasure of their marvellous company.

**Staying in . . .** is boring at worst, blissful at best.

# Libra

Librans are the most popular signs of the zodiac and, along with Ariens, are Numero Uno party people! Even when they don't really want to go out, it doesn't take much to persuade them.

**Perfect party:** Librans aren't keen on noise, so a quiet party at a hired room in a restaurant with twenty to thirty friends, some nice music and scrumptious scoff would do just fine.

**Craziest party stunt:** Dancing on the table, clad in nowt but a feather boa!

**Going out . . .** is fun but can be tiring.

**Staying in . . .** is great in the right company.

# Scorpio

When it comes to parties, Scorpians like to do the arranging and don't like anyone else interfering. They're good hosts and make polite guests. But however they choose to socialize, they'll always have a good time.

**Perfect party:** An evening at home. Food may not be a feature, but a Scorpio's guests won't be hungering for fun and games, that's for sure!

**Craziest party stunt:** Letting out a bottom burp during a game of Twister!! (Oops!)

**Going out . . .** can be fun – but only if *they've* organized everything.

**Staying in . . .** means it's time to get to grips with a good book.

# Sagittarius

Sagittarians were made for partying. If there's a party on, they don't care where it is – they're there! They have a big reputation for getting even the sleepiest of parties going and are always in hot demand as guests.

**Perfect party:** Any party – anywhere!

**Craziest party stunt:** Travelling 500 miles to a party that wasn't actually on. (Oh dear.)

**Going out . . .** is their reason for living.

**Staying in . . .** is totally soul-destroying.

# Capricorn

Partying is way down a Capricorn's list of priorities. If they *do* go out, they like to decide exactly where they're going, who they're seeing and what they're doing. Someone else's party may be full of too many surprises.

**Perfect party:** Home alone with a box of popcorn, a pile of magazines and the phone.

**Craziest party stunt:** Forgetting to bolt the toilet door.

**Going out** . . . is OK on special occasions.

**Staying in** . . . is OK any time.

# Aquarius

Although they're very sociable, Aquarians aren't really that bothered about partying. They turn down more party invitations than any other sign because, in their view, they've usually got something more interesting to do.

**Perfect party:** A Green one. (We're talking politics here.)

**Craziest party stunt:** Riding down the stairs on a trike!

**Going out** . . . should have a purpose.

**Staying in** . . . is something they should do more of.

# Pisces

Pisceans are laugh-a-minute party people and can bop till they drop! The Piscean attitude to socializing is forever changing though: sometimes they're positively agoraphobic; other times, they just *have* to go out.

**Perfect party:** At a club with a few close friends.

**Craziest party stunt:** Being wheeled home in a shopping trolley!

**Going out** . . . with a Piscean can be dangerous!

**Staying in** . . . is something they really need to do on occasion.

# Aries

Ariens are the absolute life and soul, and the most wanted guest in town! They have the ability to turn a cosy gathering into a crazy party – they customize the atmosphere to suit themselves. And they couldn't care less what anyone thinks.

**Perfect party:** An all-night do in a massive club full of thousands of ravers – all close mates, of course!

**Craziest party stunt:** Performing their own version of *Saturday Night Fever* with a mate – in their undies!

**Going out** . . . is what weekends are for!

**Staying in** . . . makes them want to go out!

# Part 9:

# Moon Magic

# Moon Rhythms

**The moon is the most feminine of the planets, and its waxing and waning affects every female on earth. Check our special chart opposite and discover how it influences you. Then use some moon magic to brighten up your life . . .**

Did you know that the human body is approximately 50 per cent water? And that in the same way that the waxing and waning moon pulls the tides of the sea, it can also have a serious pull on our bodies and minds. As the female of the species, we're even more fluid, what with periods and our ability to retain water. Because of this, our health and emotions are closely connected to the phases of the moon. Check the chart opposite and see when the moon's doing what from now till the end of the year 2000 . . .

## The Waning Phase

During the **waning phase** (the period between a Full and a New Moon), you'll be at your most serious and probably your quietest. Time should be spent in a meditative way. Many people – females in particular – feel a bit grumpy around this time and are more prone to sulking than usual. You may find it hard to relax, even though that's exactly what you *should* be doing. Quite often, you'll find that you're very forgetful around this time. If this phase coincides

|  | WANING | NEW MOON | WAXING | FULL MOON |
|---|---|---|---|---|
| **1999** | | | | |
| Sep/Oct | 26th–8th | 9th | 10th–23rd | 24th |
| Oct/Nov | 25th–7th | 8th | 9th–22nd | 23rd |
| Nov/Dec | 24th–6th | 7th | 8th–21st | 22nd |
| Dec/Jan | 23rd–5th | 6th | 7th–20th | 21st |
| | | | | |
| **2000** | | | | |
| Jan/Feb | 22nd–4th | 5th | 6th–18th | 19th |
| Feb/Mar | 20th–5th | 6th | 7th–19th | 20th |
| Mar/Apr | 21st–3rd | 4th | 5th–17th | 18th |
| Apr/May | 19th–3rd | 4th | 5th–17th | 18th |
| May/Jun | 19th–1st | 2nd | 3rd–15th | 16th |
| Jun/Jul | 17th–30th | 1st | 2nd–15th | 16th |
| Jul/Aug | 17th–30th | 31st | 1st–14th | 15th |
| Aug/Sep | 16th–28th | 29th | 30th–12th | 13th |
| Sep/Oct | 14th–26th | 27th | 28th–12th | 13th |
| Oct/Nov | 14th–26th | 27th | 28th–10th | 11th |
| Nov/Dec | 12th–24th | 25th | 26th–10th | 11th |
| Dec | 12th–24th | 25th | | |

with your pre-period days, everyone had best keep out of your way – you're a total ogre!

*When the moon's in its waning phase . . .*

. . . spend more time with your family and less with your friends

. . . rely less on others and more on your own intuition and instincts

. . . operations carried out will be very successful

. . . you're less likely to put on weight (chow down that choc!)

. . . household chores are less of a chore!

### What to do
- If you're feeling stressed, do something about it.
- Avoid negative thinking and try to develop a more positive attitude.
- Give yourself some time alone. Take a long bath, listen to some soothing music or have a bit of a cry.
- If you really don't want to be alone, make a date with someone you love and have a good cuddle!

## The New Moon
On the day of the **New Moon** (when the moon occupies the same sign as the Sun), you may have new beginnings on your mind. You feel extra energetic and may feel more driven or competitive than usual.

### At the time of the New Moon . . .

. . . you're more chatty than usual

. . . your concentration levels are up

. . . people – girls mainly – are in a more optimistic mood

. . . you're keen to get on (procrastinators and slowcoaches will really bug you!)

. . . animals and plants thrive particularly well

. . . your body is especially strong and more resistant than usual to illness

. . . you'll have more success if you make an effort to give up any bad habits you might have

. . . you're more likely to succeed at anything you attempt

### What to do

• Don't waste time – there's loads to do, so get on with it!

• Spend time with your girl friends and chat about your needs and desires. (Remember – they'll be affected by the New Moon in much the same way as you are. And you'll have a real psychic connection with mates who share your star sign.)

• Get up early, go for walks, catch up on your letter writing and make phone calls (especially the ones you've been putting off).

• Do some gardening!

• Take up a new hobby or pastime.

• Move house.

• Have another go at something you've previously failed to master. (You're sure to get the hang of it this time.)

• Grab all opportunities.

• Make up with a mate.

• Tune in to your psychic powers!

• Fall in love!

### The Waxing Phase

The **waxing**, or first phase, of the moon (the period when the moon appears to grow from what looks like a little piece

of toenail clipping to a big round dinner plate) is generally a very positive time.

*When the moon's in its waxing phase . . .*
. . . healing of wounds is slower than usual
. . . you're more likely to put on weight if you're careless about what you eat
. . . water retention and PMT are more likely to occur
. . . reactions to toxins are more dramatic

*What to do*
• Make big decisions.
• Make plans and set yourself goals. This may not be easy but any serious efforts made during these two weeks will almost definitely pay off.

## The Full Moon

When the Sun and Moon are in opposite signs of the zodiac and the moon is as round as it can possibly be, it's said to be a **Full Moon**. At this time of the month, regardless of your own personal cycle, you're likely to be more energetic than usual. If you need to tie up any loose ends, do it while the moon is on full beam. In astrology, the Full Moon often indicates the end of a chapter of your life. It can be a sad time, but it's also a time when the old makes way for the new. The Full Moon often indicates that some fab new experiences are coming your way. You should be at your most confident and self-assured and determined enough to

succeed in whatever way you want to succeed.

### At the time of the Full Moon . . .
. . . you're more likely to sleepwalk
. . . if you cut yourself, you'll bleed more than usual
. . . your period (if you're having one at the time) will be heavier
. . . you're more likely to give birth (if you're pregnant, that is)

### What to do
- Surround yourself with bright colours and with people you love.
- Involve yourself in activities that are fun but don't cost too much.
- The Full Moon is a great time for partying! So party!
- Sort out your money problems.
- Expect good news.
- Make some changes at home.
- End that so-called romance (especially if you don't even like the bloke that much).
- Face up to the truth.

## Moon Superstitions And Omens
- Never plant anything during the moon's waning phase – it won't grow to its full potential.
- The best time to get a haircut is on the day of the New Moon. Book that appointment now!
- The best marriages start just after a Full Moon.
- A baby born at the Full Moon will grow up to be very

strong. It's also said that if a moon is shining at the time of birth, the baby will be a boy; if there's no moon it'll be a girl. (Never mind genetics, eh?)

- If you steal anything on the third day after a New Moon, you'll most definitely be caught.

- To dream of the Full Moon foretells happiness in love; to dream of the waxing moon means a change for the better; dreaming of the waning moon indicates a change for the worse.

- It's reckoned that the moon can be used to forecast the weather. For example, if the moon is surrounded by a single misty ring, rain's on its way; several circles around the moon predict wet and stormy weather; if the New Moon falls on a Monday (as it did in November 1996 and April and September 1997), it signifies good news and good weather; and if the moon is bright yellow in a cloudless sky, good weather is imminent. Who needs Michael Fish when you've got the Man in the Moon?!

- There are many stories about who the "man in the moon" actually is. The Chinese say he's an old man who binds married couples with silken cord; the Masai of Kenya say he's not a man at all, but a woman with swollen lips and a missing eye – injuries inflicted upon her by her husband, the Sun; and some Germans believe he's an old man who has offended God and is eternally imprisoned on the moon. Quite.

- Turning silver over at the time of a New Moon encourages money to come your way. So check your chart and get flipping!

# Part 10:

# Your Year Ahead: The Year 2000 At A Glance

**Jan 1 2000**

*The coming twelve months are an action-packed time for Taureans.* *With eclipses in January and July; Jupiter changing signs in February and June; and Saturn making transits in August and October, you can expect major happenings galore! For each month of the year, you get a monthly feature, an in-depth week-by-week analysis, as well as an at-a-glance weekly chart to make planning ahead easier. Have a happy year!*

## JANUARY 2000

### New Year, New You!

*Stuck for New Year resolution ideas? Then get a load of these . . .*

As a **Taurean**, you know just how clumsy, stubborn and lazy you can be. So if you want to make some improvements, the question is: where do you start? Any resolution will do really . . .

**Geminians** are always flitting around, calling people they don't like in the slightest "daaarling" and kissing the air. So, really, their New Year's resolution should be to stop being so superficial. NOW!

**Cancerians** never stop droning on about their terrible lot in life. So the best New Year resolution for a moany old crab? To stop blubbing over nothing and being such an old drama queen!

**Leos** are too bossy for their own pants. If they're going to make a New Year resolution, they should remember not to treat other people like servants. (Unless they ask very nicely, of course . . .)

**Virgoans** love pick, pick, picking holes. If they're not careful, everything around them will soon look rather colander-like. Their New Year resolution should be to at least *try* saying nice things to people occasionally.

**Librans** are lazy lunks and should resolve to get up out of the midden they live in and have a darn good spring-clean. And they should have a bath while they're at it!

**Scorpians** should make an effort to be more trusting. They're so paranoid they think everyone's out to get them. Their New Year's resolution? To start believing that a lot of people really *do* have faith in them.

**Sagittarians** have enormous big mouths, which they are forever putting their huge size 12s in! The Saggie resolution for the coming year should be to be less "honest" – and to get their feet surgically trimmed. (Only joking . . . about the feet, that is!)

**Capricornians** secretly love putting a damper on other people's high spirits. They also love saying "no" for the sake of it. Their New Year's resolution for the year 2000 must be to say "yes, please" instead of "oooh, not for me thanks – I'm trying to give up" once in a while.

**Aquarians** like being cool, but sometimes they go below freezing point. They should try being more cuddly and affectionate this year.

**Pisceans** never know when to stop. In the year 2000, all Pisceans, should make "I think I've gone far enough now, thanks" their own personal slogan. (And get a T-shirt printed if necessary.)

## Key to Symbols

**LOVE:**

Snog overload

Kiss him with caution

Not a lotta totty

**FRIENDS:**

Little Miss Popular

All's fine and dandy

Watch what you say

**SOCIAL LIFE:**

Prepare to partee!

Stay cool – don't overdo it

Time to stay in 'n' chill

**Ariens** are impatient little tykes and should stop drumming their fingers on table tops and hopping from foot to foot in bus queues and try to chill out a bit this year.

## JANUARY FORECAST

### 1st–7th

An excellent aspect to Saturn in Taurus makes the first week of January the best time to get ready to face all the challenges that await you this year. Work out a plan and stick to it. The same goes for your New Year's resolutions (see the January feature "New Year, New You!"). A transiting Mars puts you at your most assertive. If there's something you want to get off your chest, now's the time to do it.

*Love:* ♡  *Friends:* 😊😊  *Social life:* 🧍

### 8th–14th

This week, the planet of responsibility Saturn changes direction in your sign, causing you to put all thoughts of selflessness aside for a moment. OK, so other people are important, but what about your own self-esteem? Think about it . . .

*Love:* ♡  *Friends:* 😊😊  *Social life:* 🧍

### 15th–21st

Mercury changes signs and your attention turns to school. You know what you're capable of, so why don't

*See page 176 for key to symbols*

you stretch yourself and prove it? If school's a bore, talk to a teacher and see if they can offer any solutions.

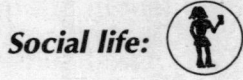

*Love:* ♡     *Friends:* 👥     *Social life:* 🕺

## 22nd–31st

The effect of the total eclipse in the communications part of your chart tells you that it's time to make some major changes to your lifestyle. News you receive before the end of the month confirms this.

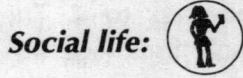

*Love:* ♡     *Friends:* 👥     *Social life:* 🕺

## FEBRUARY 2000

## Funny Valentines

*Did you know that your star sign determines the sort of Valentine you'd make? Look up your sign and check whether you'll be giving or receiving (or both) this February 14th.*

As a **Taurean**, you are extremely romantic and very sensual. Not only will you be buying your Valentine flowers and jewels, but you'll probably stretch to a jar of chocolate body paint too. Mmmm... delish!

**Geminians** think V. Day is v. exciting, but only if they get tons of cards from secret admirers. The thing is though – they're so busy thinking about themselves,

*See page 176 for key to symbols*

they clean forget to buy anything for their paramours. (Oops!)

**Cancerians** are extremely romantic and will be arranging all sorts of lovely slushy surprises for their darling. A candlelit dinner, a stroll in the moonlight and snogs a-plenty – that's what they'll be giving their sweetheart on V. Day.

**Leos** are madly extravagant and love to splash out on their loved ones. The trouble is that they do need a bit of a nudge sometimes. If a lovestruck someone dropped them a line (or a hint) prior to the big day, they'd be only too happy to oblige with love gifts a-plenty. Otherwise, they might not bother . . .

**Virgoans** are a bit stingy, so if the person they love is waiting by their letterbox for flowers, choccies and heart-shaped cushions with balloons attached with loads of love from a Virgoan paramour, they could be waiting a very long time indeed!

**Librans** are just about the silliest, slushiest, most romantic sign of the zodiac. If a lissome and lovely Libran was to be your Valentine, they'd go the whole hog, don a frilly apron and be your love slave for the day, whether that's what you wanted or not . . .

**Scorpians** love all the mystery, intrigue and question marks that surround Valentine's Day. But because they don't have a deep need to be appreciated (they actually get quite embarrassed when people get all grateful), anyone who receives a card from a Scorpian will never, ever know who it's from . . .

**Sagittarians** don't expect to get any cards and only send them if they're under immense pressure. They're notoriously lazy and unreliable too. If someone paid them a lot of money, maybe they'd send one. But then again, maybe they still wouldn't bother.

**Capricornians** will always send V. Day gifts (on the right day too!), but they don't like to buy anything too expensive, too tacky or too imaginative. Looks like a nice box of chocs is the order of the day then . . .

**Aquarians** like to throw Valentine's Day parties, then pretend they forgot it was Valentine's Day, then get loads of cards and love gifts from all their guests and not give out any themselves. Very clever . . .

**Pisceans** are real old sops: they not only pen the verses in the cards they send, but they also make the cards themselves out of a pair of their old frilly pants. Then they write a song, record it on a cassette, sellotape it inside the card and send the whole shiboodle to their "cherie amour". (Pass the sick bucket please . . . )

**Ariens** are sexy but not particularly romantic. They prefer saucy underwear to a 'ickle teddy bear with "I Wuv Oo" embroidered on its furry tum. If they actually *remember* V. Day, they'll probably forget the card, flowers and chocs and buy their loved one something small and frothy instead (and we're not talking milkshakes here).

# FEBRUARY FORECAST

## 1st–7th

The New Moon bodes well for work, so after a tough time, expect to be top of the class this week! If you're taking any tests or exams, you'll do especially well. Entering competitions is well-starred too, so give that a try if you can squeeze it in between all the school work!

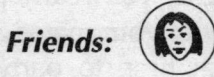

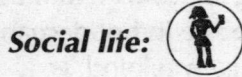

*Love:* ♡     *Friends:* 👩     *Social life:* 🕴

## 8th–14th

Mercury in the friends part of your chart causes you to ask whether certain mates really have your interests at heart. It also makes you question whether you really have the same beliefs as your mates: if you haven't, why do you pretend you do? Mars changes signs: beware of jealousy and steer clear of anyone you feel intuitively unsure of. Someone younger than you – a Geminian or a Virgoan most likely – sends you a Valentine's Day card. Any idea who that might be?

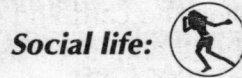

*Love:* ♡♡     *Friends:* 👥     *Social life:* 🏃

## 15th–21st

Jupiter in Taurus sees you entering an important – not to mention lucky – phase of your life. Stay optimistic and things will go from good to better. With gorgeous planet Venus getting cosy in the power part of your chart, everything's going your way. Make the most of your looks and charm – these qualities alone could win

*See page 176 for key to symbols*

you big prizes. Add them to your other talents and you can't fail! It's time to make some money too, so squeeze this week for all it's worth!

**Love:** (♡♡) **Friends:** (👭) **Social life:** (🏃)

## 22nd–29th

As the Sun changes signs, you really perk up a treat! You're in hot demand with your mates and the boys, so this weekend is a great time to party. Meeting new people and taking on new hobbies are well-starred too. So go for it! (You won't be disappointed.)

**Love:** (♡♡) **Friends:** (👭) **Social life:** (🏃)

## MARCH 2000

### Don't Forget Mother's Day!

*March is for mums – so don't forget to buy her something gorgeous on M. Day itself. If you're stuck for ideas, consider these . . .*

**Arien** mums aren't as frumpy as they sometimes look and would be quite distressed if you bought them a nice oven glove or apron for Mother's Day. Buy them the latest Verve CD though and they'd be well flattered.

**Taurean** mums are very practical and like gardening, so a nice trowel would be the ideal Mother's Day gift.

*See page 176 for key to symbols*

They're also partial to a bit of chocolate, so a *chocolate* trowel would be even better.

**Geminian** mums like surprises and would hate anything as clichéd as flowers or chocolates. They love a good read – nothing too heavy, mind – and would really appreciate an annual subscription to a posh magazine.

**Cancerian** mums are real home lovers, so anything for the house would be a good gift. Food goes down a treat – especially the gourmet variety – as does a nice leafy plant. Easy to please or what?

**Leo** mums aren't too bothered about what pressie you actually buy them: as long as it's BIG, they'll be totally impressed by it. They also like anything glittery, shiny or sparkly – never mind the quality, it's the size and the UV factor that matters.

**Virgoan** mums just *love* tidying up. They like their bodies, homes and cars to be sweet-smelling and clean at all times. If your ma's a Virgo, buy her a nice bar of soap, a mini-vac or a Magic Tree air freshener for the car.

**Libran** mums adore being fussed over and love receiving cards (home-made ones are their faves). On Mother's Day, tell her she looks gorgeous and that you love her, then present her with your latest artistic masterpiece. She'll be completely chuffed.

**Scorpian** mums like curling up on the sofa with a good book. For Mother's Day, find out her favourite author and buy her a copy of his/her most recent novel. (Make sure she hasn't got it already though. Scorpio mums have a sneaky habit of buying books on the quiet.)

**Sagittarian** mums really aren't fussy about what presents they get. As far as they're concerned, it's the thought that counts. If you remember Mother's Day at all, they'll be over the moon. And if you can't stretch to a costly gift, a big kiss and a "love you, Mum" will do just fine.

**Capricornian** mums, it has to be said, are slightly martyrish. They'll say (well in advance of Mother's Day) "No, really, Mother's Day – pah! I don't believe in it – I'd be much happier if you didn't get me anything . . . " but then they get really upset when you do as you're told. So ignore what she says. Make a big fuss of her. Make her a cake. Buy her flowers. It'll make your life a lot easier all round.

**Aquarian** mums are pretty charitable types. If you told her you weren't going to buy her a Mother's Day present, but that you were going to donate some money to her favourite charity instead, she'd be well impressed. But secretly she'd be equally thrilled with a comedy video, CD or diary.

**Piscean** mums are dreamy and romantic, and really look forward to Mother's Day. Make it worth waiting for by presenting her with a book of romantic poetry, a bottle of champagne or a big bunch of lilies. Whatever you buy, make sure it's wrapped nicely – Pisceans love a bit of fancy wrapping.

# MARCH FORECAST

### 1st–7th

With the New Moon joining the Sun in the social part of your chart, you don't intend to get involved with anything you might consider dull. Planning for the future excites you this week, especially when you meet someone who could be a massive help to you . . .

*Love:* ⬡  *Friends:* 😊  *Social life:* 🧍

### 8th–14th

With Venus in the friends part of your chart, you're in for some fun and mischief. All your worries melt away and your mates (Taurean and Libran ones in particular) are extra supportive.

*Love:* ♡  *Friends:* 😊  *Social life:* 🏃

### 15th–21st

You feel you've got it all sussed, until the end of the week, when the Sun makes its monthly transit and leaves you feeling all insecure again. The Full Moon on the 20th could mean the end of a budding romance, but sadly you knew it was a destination-nowhere thing from the start anyway, so you're hardly surprised.

*Love:* ♡  *Friends:* 😊  *Social life:* 🧍

*See page 176 for key to symbols*

### 22nd–31st

Mars in Taurus from the 23rd gives you a whole load of energy. Make sure you get out and about – and use your energy wisely. If you don't, you could come down with a nasty lurgy or even have an accident (beware all hot and sharp objects).

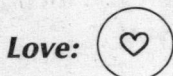

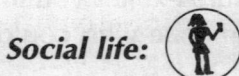

**Love:** ♡   **Friends:** 👭   **Social life:** 💃

### APRIL 2000

## Are You An Easter Chick?

*The Easter hols are here, which means lots of choc and no school. Great! Not so great though is the constant round of visiting relatives and night after night of tedious TV. Read on to discover whether Easter is your "thing" . . .*

As a **Taurean**, your favourite part of the Easter break is all the lovely chocolate! You're determined to eat as many Easter eggs as is humanly possible and then spend the rest of the hols feeling bilious. Mmm . . . fun . . .

**Geminians** like the excitement surrounding Easter but, unless they're religious types, can't really understand what all the fuss is about. If the Easter Bunny was real though . . . now that'd be a different matter altogether.

186

*See page 176 for key to symbols*

**Cancerians** love a nice family get-together, so if there are any rellos visiting or to be visited, Cancer will be in their element. The best bit about Easter, as far as they're concerned, is all the home-made cakes (especially the hot cross buns). Yum!

**Leos** see Easter as an opportunity to buy their nearest and dearest some lovely choccy gifts. It's a little-known astrological fact that most people who shop at Thornton's over the Easter period are Leos. (Maybe.)

**Virgoans** think Easter is a silly and frivolous waste of time. In their opinion, it's a waste of valuable school time and if they had their way, there wouldn't be any Easter holidays at all. (The summer hols would be extended by two weeks instead.)

**Librans** like everything to do with Easter – the cards, the Easter eggs, the "Jesus" films on TV and the family gatherings. Why it's just like Christmas, but with daffodils and bunnies and little fluffy yellow chicks. (OK, that's enough, Libra!)

**Scorpians** really like the fact that everything goes a bit quiet over Easter and that they can relax for a short moment in their otherwise hectic lives. Trouble is, year after year, they always invite tons of relatives round for celebratory drinks and snacks, thus making Easter more hard work than any other time of year. And they never learn either . . .

**Sagittarians,** unless deeply religious, couldn't give a monkey's about Easter. They're more than likely to use the time off to go somewhere as far away from home as possible (somewhere they don't celebrate Easter preferably . . .)

**Capricornians** don't particularly like Easter but feel it's their duty to celebrate it. This means doing all the traditional stuff associated with the festival, such as baking hot cross buns, giving (and scoffing) Easter eggs, and having people round for tea. Then moaning about it. A lot.

**Aquarians** like having time off from school, but aren't overly bothered about celebrating Easter in the traditional way. No, they're more likely to use the hols as a time to catch up on the soaps, read a couple of books and update their diary.

**Pisceans** enjoy privacy, so the thought of a whole barrage of relatives coming over for Easter Sunday lunch sends shivers up their sensitive little spines. Ideally, they'd spend the hols lolling around in a negligee, daintily munching on a few Milk Tray and saying "I want to be alone".

**Ariens** love the holidays, but can't abide Easter itself. It's the crap telly that upsets them the most. All those variety performances! Breaking up from school is fab – there's no denying that. But it's all downhill after that really.

## APRIL FORECAST

### 1st–7th

Don't think someone's trying to pull an April Fool's Day stunt when a gorgeous bloke makes it known that he wants to get to know you better. It's for real – and deep down you know it is – so go for it!

**Love:** **Friends:** **Social life:**

## 8th–14th
A transiting Mercury means you refuse to believe anything unless you hear it straight from the horse's mouth. Gossip is of no interest to you: there are far more important things to think about right now – like yourself! (*Sooo* Taurean!)

**Love:** **Friends:** **Social life:**

## 15th–21st
As the Sun enters Taurus, you're feeling utterly fab. The new love in your life helps of course, but you'd be feeling confident even without this influence. You're the girl everyone wants to hang out with, and you're looking gorgeous too! What an excellent week! (Even better if it's your birthday!)

**Love:** **Friends:** **Social life:**

## 22nd–30th
With an amazing six planets – the Sun, Mercury, Venus, Mars, Jupiter and Saturn – in Taurus by the end of the month, you're in high spirits but rather restless. Put your energy into catching up with your school work.

**Love:** **Friends:** **Social life:**

*See page 176 for key to symbols*

## MAY 2000

### Spring Fever!

*At this time of the year, all the signs of the zodiac tend to get a tad frisky. Some more than others . . .*

As a **Taurean**, you know for sure that you always feel the effects of the spring. But the only action you're likely to take is to swap your 13-tog duvet for a 10-tog one, then to snuggle back down . . .

**Geminians** go ever so slightly bonkers when the spring kicks in. All they want to do is go out and have a good time. (So what's new then?)

**Cancerians** are seriously affected by the spring, in that all they can think about is redecorating. Come May, there's a huge increase in the number of folk hanging out at B&Q, and, guess what – most of them are Cancerians. Allegedly.

**Leos,** at the first sign of warm weather, start stripping off and baring their bods to the sunshine. They don't actually care if the rest of the world is still wearing its anorak – a string vest and Bermuda shorts will do Leo just fine.

**Virgoans** go mad in the spring all right. All they want to do is spring-clean. "That spring sunshine doesn't half show up the dust," you'll hear them say at least twelve times a day, as they gad about brandishing a feather duster.

**Librans** find this time of year the most romantic time of all. If they don't go actively looking for love in May, then they'll hole themselves up at home with a big stack of weepy black-and-white movies and a pile of lace hankies, and get soppy on their own instead.

**Scorpians** are a sexy bunch, and start to feel their sap rising at the mere mention of spring. Almost all of the opposite sex become irresistibly attractive to Scorpians at this time of year and many of them start a passionate romance in May. Come summer though, they realize what a mistake they've made. (Oops!)

**Sagittarians** get itchy feet (and we're not talking athlete's foot here) in the spring and can't wait to get away. Many of them *have* to wait though, so at this time of year their craziness isn't due so much to spring fever, as to the fact that they can't do as they want.

**Capricornians** are *never* crazy: they're just too sensible to let anything – spring included – make them behave out of character. They might – just *might* – turn up the volume on their transistor radio a smidgen, but that's about as far as it goes.

**Aquarians** are pretty crazy at the best of times, so the time of year doesn't really make much difference. Spring sometimes brings out their creative side though, and many an Aquarian will be seen sporting a beret and brandishing a paintbrush in May.

**Pisceans** would spend the whole of spring in Paris if they could – it's just *sooo* romantic there (so they've heard). If they haven't a paramour at this time of year, they'll spend every waking hour searching for one. Spring fever at its worst . . .

**Ariens** are seriously affected by the warmer weather and can go a bit crazy if not carefully monitored. Arien females can't get enough of the boys at this time of year and seem to fancy every single one they see. Careful now . . .

## MAY FORECAST

### 1st–7th

With six planets in Taurus until the 4th (when Mars changes signs – a good thing because that'll make you less accident-prone after this date), this could be one of the best weeks of the year. If it's your birthday, it'll be even better!! Brace yourself for fun and romance galore.

*Love:*  *Friends:*  *Social life:*

### 8th–14th

Mercury in Taurus could make you rather fidgety, which doesn't help anything much. Mars settled in the money part of your chart means you could come up with some money-spinning ideas. If you do, act quick before someone else nicks them.

*Love:*  *Friends:*  *Social life:*

### 15th–21st

With Mercury joining your ruling planet Venus in your

*See page 176 for key to symbols*

sign this week, you're in a hyper-sociable mood. Spend as much time as you can with people you love, but try not to neglect your school work. People are queuing up to be your mate and you're the first name on everybody's party list (even your own if you're throwing a "do" of the b.day variety!). The Full Moon in your opposite signs marks a change in your love life. It seems you both want each other, but something (or someone) is getting in the way. Try to be patient – a solution is about to be found.

*Love:*     *Friends:*     *Social life:* 

## 22nd–31st

The Sun joins Mars and Mercury, which puts you in a top money-making mood. Trouble is, you're easily distracted and may miss out on really obvious opportunities. Keep your eyes open and your ear to the ground if you want to feed your piggy-bank!

*Love:*     *Friends:*     *Social life:* 

## JUNE 2000

### . . . And Don't Forget Father's Day Either!

*If you want to buy your Dad a special gift on Father's Day, why bother when he'd much rather you did something else? Want to know more? Then keep reading . . .*

*See page 176 for key to symbols*

**Arien** dads quite like the idea of Father's Day. In fact, they like the idea of anything that means they're the focus of everyone's attention. If your Pop's an Arien, he's no exception. He's not bothered about pressies though – he'd much rather you challenged him to a game of footie down the park.

**Taurean** dads find all that Father's Day malarkey a bit embarrassing and would prefer it if you just let him have an extra long lie-in – all day preferably – then brought him the papers and a nice cup of tea. (Aw, he doesn't ask for much, does he?)

**Geminian** dads aren't usually around much, but they'd really appreciate a phone call (wherever they might be). Cheap if he's in Bognor – a tidy sum if he's in Bangladesh!

**Cancerian** dads love photos, so take him down to the photo booth at Woolies, get a strip of funny "instant" pics of you and him pulling funny faces, and stick 'em in a photo album. A lovely and unusual gift that costs not very much.

**Leo** dads like their kids to appreciate them. Usually they like really big, expensive presents, but if you could spend the whole of Father's Day telling him what a top bloke he is and how he's the best dad in the cosmiverse, you could save yourself a whole load of cash.

**Virgoan** dads enjoy intellectual pursuits, so on Father's Day, instead of buying him a mug with "The World's

No. 1 Dad" emblazoned on it, pretend you're Magnus Magnusson and invite him to appear on your own special edition of *Mastermind*. (He'll think he's in heaven!)

**Libran** dads love people doing things for them. On Father's Day, ask him if there's anything he wants doing and he's sure to present you with a big, long list. After cleaning the car, polishing his shoes (all of them) and filing all his bills, you'll be fed up, but he'll have had a nice time.

**Scorpian** dads love winning so, on Father's Day, challenge him to a game of Scrabble or three and let him win. He'll be *sooo* happy!

**Sagittarian** dads love a pint. So take him down the pub and give him a couple of quid to buy himself one. (If you're under age and not allowed in, you can sit outside in the car with a bag of crisps and a bottle of pop till he's finished.)

**Capricornian** dads really enjoy curries. They're a bit expensive from the local takeaway mind, so why not attempt to make your own from ingredients already in your kitchen cupboard? Look to your mum's Madhur Jaffrey cookbook for inspiration . . .

**Aquarian** dads really like dancing. The only problem is, they're not very good at it and usually end up looking like right plonkers! On Father's Day, allow him to dance to his heart's content – and *don't* laugh (not even a little bit).

**Piscean** dads' preferred pastime is watching videos. On Father's Day, hire a few of his all-time fave movies and let him watch them till his eyes go square. Then return the vids to the hire shop for him: that's the bit he hates most.

## JUNE FORECAST

### 1st–7th

With three planets *and* the New Moon in the money part of your chart this week, there's no avoiding facing up to cash matters. You're in a positive mood, so try to cash in on your talents. Writing could prove profitable. Try it and see.

*Love:* ♡  *Friends:* 😊  *Social life:* 🕺

### 8th–14th

This week marks the beginning of a prosperous phase for all Taureans. You won't be rolling in it exactly, but you'll have more dosh than you thought you would have at this point in time. You may have a desire to be flash with your cash, but avoid this or you'll be broke again before you know it.

*Love:* 💕  *Friends:* 😊  *Social life:* 🕺

### 15th–21st

The Sun, Mercury and Venus in the communications section of your chart make you enthusiastic, confident and energetic. Being seen in the right places and

*See page 176 for key to symbols*

hanging out with the right people will bring about solutions to pressing problems. Brilliant news from a relative makes this an extra-special week.

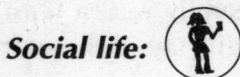

**Love:** (♡)   **Friends:** (image)   **Social life:** (image)

## 22nd–30th

As the Sun changes signs, you're full of enthusiasm and confidence. You shine most at parties, so get to as many as you can. Mercury starts going backwards through the money part of your chart and this warns you to be careful if you're thinking about lending or investing any cash.

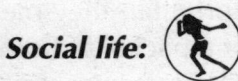

**Love:** (♡♡)   **Friends:** (image)   **Social life:** (image)

## JULY 2000

## What Sort Of Shopper Are You?

*Now the summer sales are on, will you be dashing out spending? Much of your shopping style depends on your star sign. For example . . .*

You **Taureans** like to take your time when you go on a spree, and enjoy making a day of it – starting early, stopping for a snack, then continuing to browse. When you find something you like, you splash out. Otherwise, that purse remains tightly shut.

*See page 176 for key to symbols*

197

**Geminians** can spend a record amount of cash in a very limited time but sometimes lose their sense of judgment in the process. They love shopping and usually return with armloads of stuff – most of which will stay in the carrier bags for ever more!

**Cancerian** folk are careful shoppers and won't buy unless they're sure they really *will* use their purchase. They don't mind spending a lot – as long as it's on themselves. Buying presents for others is *not* their speciality by any stretch of the imagination.

**Leo** shoppers are wildly extravagant – always ready to treat themselves and others – and will always spend far more than they mean to. In fact, if someone goes out for a packet of Rolos and comes back with half of Miss Selfridge, chances are they're a Leo.

**Virgoans** are extremely fussy and, when shopping, will to and fro between shops for hours. Unless the potential purchase is perfect in every way and has a myriad of uses, they won't buy it. Fact: Virgoans are the shoppers most likely to return home empty-handed.

**Librans** like shopping and can be extravagant when the mood takes them. They're real ditherers, though, and because they find it hard to make up their minds, they often buy everything in sight (just in case) and end up very confused – not to mention broke.

**Scorpians** – males and females alike – have a reputation for being careful with their cash but they secretly love to spend, saving their money, then blowing it all in a single day! Big purchases appeal most – the more expensive, the better.

**Sagittarians** shop in a most haphazard fashion, and can spend hours running about, not knowing what they want or what to buy. They buy a lot of things that they think will come in handy, but most of the stuff they come home with is, in fact, pretty useless.

**Capricornians** are the most cautious shoppers of all and don't really like to part with their hard-earned dosh, preferring instead to save it all up. Purchases are made only when necessary, and the word "spree" doesn't actually feature in their vocabulary. And, although prudent, they're the most likely sign to avoid the sales.

**Aquarians** can be a tad antisocial and would rather do their shopping by mail order than fighting the high street crowds. Computer-literate Aquarians surf the Internet and shop that way – then get the goods delivered to their door. More civilized by far!

**Pisceans** are daydreamers. They tend to get an idea of what it is they want to buy, then spend most of their lives looking for it. Chances are, their dream purchase doesn't actually exist! But because they love browsing, they don't really care.

**Arien** shoppers are incredibly impatient. You won't be found waiting in a long queue to pay for *anything* – not even the world's best bargain. They're naturally impulsive too, which means they've got a wardrobe-full of purchases that never should have been.

## JULY FORECAST

### 1st–7th

With four planets *and* the New Moon in the communications part of your chart this week, you can't fail to impress everyone you meet. If you've an interview of any kind lined up, you'll do exceptionally well; parties are well-starred; and you're feeling daring enough to go your own way and not go along with everyone else. What a girl!

*Love:* ⬭  *Friends:* ◉  *Social life:* ◉

### 8th–14th

With Jupiter now settled in the money part of your chart, you're easily impressed by other people's cash and possessions. Keeping up with your more spendthrifty mates is top priority to you right now, even if you know you can't really do it. You'd be better off saving your dosh – even if it does make you a bit of a wet blanket.

*Love:* ◯  *Friends:* ◉  *Social life:* ◉

### 15th–21st

This week's eclipse causes travel problems and delays. If you're going on a family holiday, don't be surprised if you have to sleep on your suitcases at the airport! You *will* get there in the end – it's just going to take longer than you envisage . . .

*See page 176 for key to symbols*

*Love:* ( ♡ )   *Friends:* ( 👩 )   *Social life:* ( 🕺 )

### 22nd–31st

The Sun and your ruler Venus in the home and family section of your chart mean all problems are resolved with close relatives (namely parents and/or siblings). In fact, being with your family is your top pastime. (Which is lucky, because you may not have much choice but to be with them.)

*Love:* ( ♡ )   *Friends:* ( 👭 )   *Social life:* ( 🏃 )

## AUGUST 2000

### Holiday Romance

***To some people, the summer is all about love. Are you the sort to indulge in a holiday romance? It all depends on your star sign . . .***

You **Taureans** want a good time and if a romance happens whilst on holiday, it's a bonus. You don't go out of your way to find a bloke, but you'll certainly indulge in a fair bit of flirting. If you take a boyfriend on holiday with you, you'll be all over each other; if you go away single, you're likely to come back in love.

**Geminians** are the biggest flirts of the zodiac. Holiday romances were made for them. The thing they like most about summer flings is their brevity and the fact that they don't have to see the bloke ever again! Few Gemini girls take a boyfriend away with them but, with or without a boyfriend in tow, Miss Gemini will have a whale of a time.

**Cancerians** often fantasize about meeting a handsome foreigner and falling in love and, because of that, holiday romance is a serious business for them. They're destined to have several romances abroad. They're convinced they're the "real thing" and are disappointed when they discover they're not. If they holiday with a boyfriend, they'll only have eyes for him; if they go in search of love, they'll find it in one form or another.

**Leos,** when they get involved with someone on holiday, enjoy the snogging but rarely fall in love. If they go away with a boyfriend, they'll spend half their time eating, the other half snogging. If they go blokeless, they make sure they have fun – and that includes dancing the night away, attempting to pull every half-decent bloke in sight!

**Virgoans** don't really like foreign affairs, but that doesn't mean they completely rule out the chance of holiday romance. They're not into casual relationships or one-night stands, and as many holiday love scenarios *are* casual, Virgoans go out of their way not to get involved. Holidaying with a boyfriend is more their thing; and they'd rather stay at home than go on holiday alone.

**Librans** love the idea of a holiday romance. A romance abroad is a romance made in heaven as far as they're concerned. Flirtatious by nature, they love the thrill of the chase and when they go on holiday, they don't stop running for a second! They tend to get involved very quickly though, and this can lead to many regrets.

**Scorpians** are sexy enough to know they can have a holiday romance if they want one, but chances are they're just not interested. They like to have a good time when they're on holiday, and having an affair just detracts from this in their opinion. They take love seriously and won't have a fling just for the fun of it. They like to holiday alone and won't stand for being pestered by any local romeos.

**Sagittarians** see holiday romances as just one of their many hobbies! If they see someone they fancy on holiday (and they usually do – on the first day more often than not!), they get to work quickly. Language differences pose no problems for them – they're quite adept at interpreting body language!

**Capricornians** go on holiday to see the sights, sample the culture and have a good time. Having a holiday fling doesn't really come into it. They're cautious by nature and believe that brief holiday encounters are quite risky. That's why they avoid them like the plague.

**Aquarians** don't often holiday in very romantic places, but if they happen to come across a bloke who shares their interests and beliefs, they won't mind seeing him once or twice during the holiday. Aquarians in a relationship may need to holiday alone; it's not just school they need a break from!

**Pisceans**, whether attached or single, are always in demand when on holiday. They're very romantic and love the idea of a holiday romance, but the passionate affair they envisage often turns out to be no more than a rather depressing one-night (or two-week) stand. If they take a boyfriend on holiday, their "grass is always greener" attitude could cause a row or two. (Yikes!)

**Ariens** love an adventure of the romantic variety and what better way to indulge than to have a holiday romance? If you go on holiday with a boyfriend, the whole thing will be a bit of a snogsome affair. If they go without a bloke, their holiday becomes one great flirtathlon!

## AUGUST FORECAST

### 1st–7th
Mercury in the communications part of your chart provides you with brilliant insight and great wit. If you need to impress anyone, you'll do it ten times over this week. In fact, you even impress *yourself* with your eloquence and charm!

**Love:** ♡   **Friends:** 👭   **Social life:** 🧍

### 8th–14th
Saturn leaves Taurus and sees you in desperate need of

*See page 176 for key to symbols*

cash. There's no point sitting around worrying about it. Stay in, save any cash that comes your way, and stop acting like a millionaire. With Mars in the home and family part of your chart, there's all manner of confusion. This should be a happy time and it *would* be if a certain male personage wasn't mucking things up for you. Don't let him get to you.

**Love:** **Friends:** **Social life:**

## 15th–21st

The Full Moon in the "power" part of your chart makes you feel a tad unappreciated. You need to show people just how clever you are, and this week you must decide how to go about doing this. Get it right and you'll get all the recognition – and appreciation – you deserve.

**Love:** **Friends:** **Social life:**

## 22nd–31st

As the Sun joins Mercury and your ruler Venus in your astrological house of fun and frolics, you're in the mood for love. Work is a definite no-no, so the thought of going back to school next week may be quite painful – especially if there's some unfinished business from the summer holidays still to be be dealt with . . . If there is, deal with it now – it could be your last chance.

**Love:** **Friends:** **Social life:**

*See page 176 for key to symbols*

## SEPTEMBER 2000

### Star Students

*September means one thing: no more summer holidays. School – depending on your star sign – brings either great sadness or great joy. Find out how you'll be feeling as the new term begins . . .*

As a **Taurean**, you progress slowly but surely with most subjects. If you want to excel in any area, though, you'll have to stop being so stubborn. Unless you pay more attention, you're destined to be a dunce. (Most frequently heard refrain from Teach: "Go and stand in the corner and don the pointy hat!")

**Geminians** are irritatingly intelligent and, although they're not particularly brilliant at any one subject, they do OK. They *will* insist on getting up to mischief in class though. (Most frequently heard refrain from Teach: "Is it something you'd like to share with the rest of the class?")

**Cancerians** are quite good students but really need to swot to get good grades. They have to be in the right mood to concentrate though (when it's a New Moon preferably), and spend many a lesson staring blankly out of the window. (Most frequently heard refrain from Teach: "What *is* it that's so interesting out there?")

**Leos** love messing about. To a Leo, lessons are annoying interruptions to the one long lunch break that is their life. If they could be bothered to come in from the playground, they'd probably do quite well. (Most frequently heard refrain from Teach: "Didn't you hear the bell, cloth-ears?")

**Virgoans** insist on doing everything in their own inimitable style. They're popular with classmates, but teachers can't abide their Norman Know-it-all ways. (Most frequently heard refrain from Teach: "Put your hand down and let someone else answer!")

**Librans** think school is a right laugh. It's where they conduct their social life. They're not so keen on the lessons though. The teachers spoil things a bit too. And as for rules – well they're fun to break, but that's all. (Most frequently heard refrain from Teach: "Could you *please* turn off that mobile phone?!")

**Scorpians** are swots. With their photographic memories, they just love remembering great long lists of dates and formulae. And as for exams – why, they're a complete doddle! (Most frequently heard refrain from Teach: "Take this certificate of merit and go to the top of the class!")

**Sagittarians** detest school. They're the naughtiest people in the class and can be extremely disruptive. They drive even the most tolerant teacher to distraction because they never, *ever* do as they're told. (Most frequently heard refrain from Teach: "What's your excuse *this* time?")

**Capricornians** are the teachers' pets of the zodiac.

They're quiet and studious, yet strangely not very bright. Despite this, all their mates copy from them. (Most frequently heard refrain from Teach: "Why has everyone else in the class got the same (wrong) answers as you?")

**Aquarians** like doing everything their own way and that doesn't go down too well with the teachers. They also love skiving. In fact, given the choice, they wouldn't bother with school at all. (Most frequently heard refrain from Teach: "Where were you yesterday during double biology?")

**Pisceans** love doodling and writing poetry. But that's about it. Ask them to do anything involving numbers, chemicals or common sense and they blow a fuse. (Most frequently heard refrain from Teach: "Recite the chemical symbol for potassium chloride and tuck those wires back in your ears!")

**Ariens** are excellent at PE. If "attention-seeking" was a subject, they'd be great at that too. If they didn't enjoy sitting in the back row of the class so much, they'd be grade A students. (Most frequently heard refrain from Teach: "Come and sit at the front right NOW!")

## SEPTEMBER FORECAST

### 1st—7th
A lovely aspect between Neptune and your ruling planet Venus helps you really tune in to the needs of your loved ones. If you want to help anyone this week,

you're well able to do it. You just have to *want* to, that's all . . .

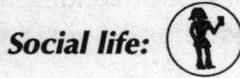

Love: (symbol)   Friends: (symbol)   Social life: (symbol)

## 8th–14th

Mercury joins Venus in the health part of your chart. You're getting stressed out and should try to take it easy if you want to avoid coming down with horrible lurgies. Stop taking on so much. This week's Full Moon suggests it's high time you took a close look at some of your so-called "mates". Some of them haven't really got your interests at heart and are only hanging out with you for selfish reasons. One friendship may have to end, but this just leaves a gap which will soon be filled someone new.

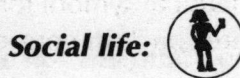

Love: (symbol)   Friends: (symbol)   Social life: (symbol)

## 15th–21st

Passion planet Mars enters the love and fun part of your chart, and you're in a lustful and lecherous mood. OK, so you should be concentrating on school (what with it being the start of the new school year and everything), but all you can think about is snogging! (Oh dear . . . )

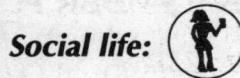

Love: (symbol)   Friends: (symbol)   Social life: (symbol)

## 22nd–30th

Love planet Venus enters your opposite sign, ensuring

that all your relationships are happy. Romance is well-starred through to the end of the month; about time too – it's been lacking lately. Be as loving and generous as possible and you'll be handsomely rewarded.

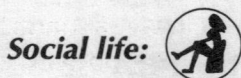

**Love:** **Friends:** **Social life:**

## OCTOBER 2000

### Halloween Horrors

*Use your psychic powers (and, yes, we all have them!), and this year's Halloween will be extra spooky!*

Note: if any of the technical terms (in italics) used below baffle you, check the glossary on page 213.

You **Taureans**, like Ariens, should also trust your instincts. Your hidden psychic ability is also *divination*, and you should concentrate on *numerology* and *dowsing* if you want to develop this talent. If you were to choose a psychic career, you'd be a *numerologist*.

**Geminians** are naturally very crafty and clever and can often fool people into believing they're psychic. In actual fact, they are pretty *telepathic* and should use this power wisely. Other areas that may fascinate them are *palmistry* and *graphology*.

**Cancerians** are highly sensitive and this is a bonus if they're considering developing any psychic talents

*See page 176 for key to symbols*

they might have. If they read up on tea leaf reading and *scrying*, they'd find it very interesting. Their secret psychic talents are *clairaudience* and *clairvoyance.*

**Leos** have a natural ability to connect with people. They're good with others on a one-to-one, face-to-face level and have a real interest in other people's lives. They sometimes have great powers of *precognition*, which can be useful. But it's astrology and tarot reading that really enthral a Leo.

**Virgoans** have extremely sharp intuition, but are rather dubious about the existence of psychic powers. They may not know this, but they actually have a powerful healing touch and would make excellent psychic healers. Next time someone close to them is feeling poorly, they should lay their hands on them and see what happens . . .

**Librans** are very understanding types and are psychically highly sensitive. Of all the signs, they're the one most likely to possess the ability to see *auras*. If they wanted a psychic career, one as an aura reader would suit them well.

**Scorpians** are fascinated by all things mysterious and this includes the world of psychic powers. With those amazing eyes and that soft voice, they'd make top hypnotists. Move over, Paul McKenna, and let Miss Scorpio take the stage!

**Sagittarians** are very open-minded and this can make them psychic in the most dramatic way. Many are *psychokinetic* and some even experience visions. If a Saggie were to choose a psychic career, they'd make a great prophet. (Well, *someone* has to do it . . !)

**Capricornians,** although quite cynical about psychic stuff, are very tolerant and would never dismiss it as a load of twaddle. What they don't realize is that they're actually pretty psychic; they just don't pay too much attention to that part of themselves, that's all. A career as a colour therapist would suit a Capricorn – it's not too spooky but good intuition is vital. Something they have by the barrowload.

**Aquarians** are extremely positive and sensitive people and are able to pick up all sorts of signs and signals that others would miss completely. They're interested in what makes other folk tick and would do well studying *biorhythms.* In fact, they could even make a career of it if they wanted . . .

**Pisceans** are the dreamers of the zodiac. And that's why so many solutions, ideas and messages come to them whilst they're in the dream state. They're also pretty clairvoyant and are the most likely sign to see a ghost or apparition. If they fancied doing something spooky for a living, a Piscean would make a fab *medium.* (Just so long as they don't frighten themselves . . . they're easily spooked!)

**Ariens** have really good natural instincts: if they get a gut feeling about something, they're usually right. If they want to develop their psychic powers, they should concentrate on seeing into the future. They're also interested in *runes* and *phrenology*. If they were a psychic by trade, they'd be a fortune-teller.

## Glossary

**Aura** = the subtle power that emanates from the body

**Biorhythms** = body "moods"

**Clairaudience** = "hearing" voices and/or sounds not perceptible to the other senses

**Clairvoyance** = the power of seeing or perceiving objects not perceptible to the other senses

**Divination** = the ability to see into the future

**Dowsing** = using a divining rod to discover underground water and/or minerals

**Graphology** = character analysis using handwriting

**Medium** = someone who can receive information from the "spirit world"

**Numerologist** = someone who studies the psychic significance of numbers

**Numerology** = the study of the significance of numbers

**Palmistry** = studying the hands and palms for character-reading and fortune-telling

**Phrenology** = character analysis using the bumps on the head!

**Precognition** = having visions of the future through dreams, ideas, feelings or visions

**Psychokinetic** = able to move objects without touching them

**Runes** = carved Scandinavian stones used for fortune-telling

**Scrying** = crystal ball reading

**Telepathic** = able to pick up and transmit thoughts without using the senses of sight, smell, hearing, taste or touch

## OCTOBER FORECAST

### 1st–7th

An aspect between the Moon and Mercury in your opposite sign suggests that, on the love front, you should stop blaming everyone else for the mess you've got yourself into. It's all your own fault. So be grown-up and take some responsibility.

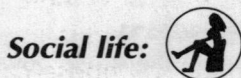

**Love:** ⊙  **Friends:** 😊  **Social life:** 🚶

## 8th–14th

This week's Full Moon is telling you that it's not what's on the surface that counts. Look further than your own and other people's appearances and you'll soon realize just how true that is. Facing up to certain truths about yourself is necessary right now. It may be painful, but it *has* to be done. So do it.

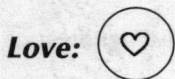

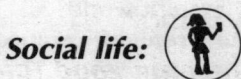

**Love:** ♡  **Friends:** 😊  **Social life:** 🧍

## 15th–21st

As Saturn moves backwards into Taurus on the 16th, you're able to make an effort to overcome that irrational fear of failure which has been plaguing you for so long now. Finally, you're aware of your capabilities and won't let anyone tell you otherwise. Believe in yourself 100 per cent (you've no reason not to), and big-time success is sure to follow.

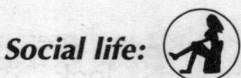

**Love:** ⊙♡  **Friends:** 😊  **Social life:** 🚶

## 22nd–31st

You're at your sexiest, thanks to the most recent Venus transit. You're a big hit with everyone you meet –

*See page 176 for key to symbols*

especially members of the opposite sex – and can use your sex appeal to get your own way in every situation (nothing new there then . . . ) You're destined to have a fab time on Halloween, providing you wear the right outfit. So choose carefully . . .

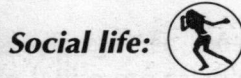

*Love:*  (symbol)   *Friends:*  (symbol)   *Social life:*  (symbol)

## NOVEMBER 2000

### Will Your Bonfire Night Go With A Bang?

*The only good thing about the dreary month of November is Bonfire Night. Totally agree? Then you must be an Taurean . . .*

You **Taureans** quite like Bonfire Night but you aren't the biggest socializer in the zodiac. At a fireworks party, you're invariably stood in the shadows, quietly scoffing baked potatoes. Copping off is a rare occurrence: your mouth's too full of grub to snog!!

**Geminians** *pretend* to like fireworks because fireworks look so cool, but deep down they're petrified of all the whizzing and banging. That's why they always find someone to snog at bonfire parties – they're much happier on a comfy sofa than in a chilly back yard!

*See page 176 for key to symbols*

**Cancerians** are always happy to help out at any sort of party, but those of the bonfire variety aren't really their favourites. They prefer edible bangers to the exploding kind and may just turn up for the scoff. And why not indeed . . . ?

**Leos**, as Fire Signs, enjoy a good firework display. They're more inclined to attend a big public show than a house party, because they like their fireworks on a grand scale. At-home bonfire "do's" always seem to disappoint them – more so if there's not enough decent totty around . . .

**Virgoans** are sticklers for everything being just so, so the mess of a bonfire party can really upset them. Whether the party is their own or someone else's, a Virgoan is the "helpful" person hoovering the carpet and sweeping the patio – and, basically, not having very much fun at all.

**Librans** love the pretty colours of the fireworks and the whole atmosphere of a cracking bonfire party. But, because of the responsibility involved, they're unlikely to throw a party of their own. So they'll just go to other people's and have fun at their expense instead.

**Scorpians** enjoy bonfire parties – the fireworks, the weather and the fact that it's so close to their birthday sets them aglow with excitement. It can make them feel rather sexy too and more likely than the other signs to cop off with someone.

**Sagittarians**, as Fire Signs, love Guy Fawkes Night. They love parties even more, so the combination of the two is fab! They love getting involved with the setting off of fireworks, but, if there are any sensible people about, Saggies may not be allowed to get their hands on anything dangerous. (They're famous for their carelessness.)

**Capricornians** reckon that fireworks are dangerous and expensive and, because of this, they're unlikely to ever throw a Bonfire Night party of their own. They may attend someone else's party, but they'll stand well clear of the fireworks and make a lot of tutting noises – much to everyone else's annoyance.

**Aquarians** think fireworks are an evil waste of money and believe that the cash spent on them every year should be used to buy far more worthy things. They're not overly keen on parties either, so probably wouldn't enjoy a bonfire do too much.

**Pisceans** hate noise and crowds: their idea of a nightmare would be a huge public fireworks display. A small party in someone's garden is bad enough, but they'll go if there's a free Lucozade to be had.

**Ariens** are a Fire signs and love a good Bonfire Night. Being ruled by Mars, they're the most likely sign to get burnt (metaphorically or physically) at a bonfire do, so they should be extra vigilant at all times and avoid lighting fireworks. They also get impatient with all the hanging around, and if a party's not well organized enough, they may even start complaining. Or take over . . .

## NOVEMBER FORECAST

### 1st–7th

Mars changes signs and your attitude towards health and lifestyle changes too. Maybe you're thinking about turning veggie or spending more time exercising. Whatever – you certainly won't be stuffing your face with lardy sausages at the Bonfire party you're going to! You've got your health and waistline to consider . . .

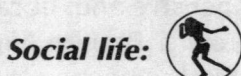

*Love:* ⬤  *Friends:* ⬤  *Social life:* ⬤

### 8th–14th

If you've been hoping to set the record straight with a certain guy, do it after the 8th, when Mercury enters your opposite sign and makes it easier to talk to people of the opposite sex. A weekend away might be a good idea – you need to take a breather.

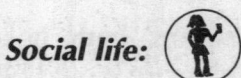

*Love:* ⬤  *Friends:* ⬤  *Social life:* ⬤

### 15th–21st

Venus in the travel part of your chart forecasts time away from home. Many Taureans will be taking an early winter holiday; others will be expanding their horizons in other ways. Whatever you do, you're likely to end up a whole lot wiser for it.

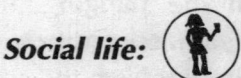

*Love:* ⬤  *Friends:* ⬤  *Social life:* ⬤

*See page 176 for key to symbols*

## 22nd–30th

A lot of the problems you're experiencing at the moment are to do with your own insecurities, and the New Moon advises you to get to the bottom of these once and for all. If you have the hots for someone, ask yourself why. You may find that you don't really fancy him after all. And that'll free you up a whole lot . . .

*Love:* (♡)    *Friends:* (☺)    *Social life:* (👤)

## DECEMBER 2000

### Cosmic Christmas Gifts

*Because, astrologically speaking, the outer and inner self are often totally different, what we want and what we actually get for Christmas are equally different. If you're wondering what gifts to buy your friends and family this year, read this first . . .*

As a **Taurean**, you tend to be viewed as a couldn't-care-less type, so people rarely put much thought into gifts for you. But you're actually quite snooty, so anything cheap 'n' nasty *won't* be well received. In fact, you'd rather have nothing than something that isn't of the highest quality. So there you have it . . . Nothing it is!

**Geminians,** although cutely kitsch on the surface, are actually – on the sneak – a bit of a class act. They'd be eternally grateful for a nice pair of suede gloves. But what do they get? Fluffy mules and a feather boa – that's what! Ta very much Santa . . .

**Cancerians** are modest types who don't ask for much. Yeah – right! Like they'd be happy with a set of hankies or a nice book! Forget it! Underneath that "no-really-I-just-don't-need-anything" exterior, lies a total pressie-grabber – the more the merrier as far as they're concerned.

**Leos** love very expensive, quality gifts. Simple, eh? So why does everyone insist on buying them such a load of old tack every Christmas? All they want is a nice little something in white gold or platinum, but no. Mates and Santa alike come bearing gifts of the see-thru nightie, nasty perfume and cheap chocs variety instead.

**Virgoans** may seem shy, but beneath that slightly inhibited surface lies a complete wild child. Ask a Virgoan what they really want for Christmas and you may well be shocked by their answer. But a gnome hat and matching scarf is about as shocking as the pressies ever get. Sad but true . . .

**Librans**, although quite fluffy on the surface, would love nothing more than a nice pair of thermal long-johns. So why do friends and relatives shower them with exotic lingerie year in year out? OK, so they may look fab in a satin g-string, but they'd much rather have something for everyday wear.

**Scorpians** are fed up with all the black tights and socks people throw their way every Christmas. It's not that they don't use them, it's just most Scorpians have at least 150 pairs! Cheer them up this year by buying them some nice pink ones instead. It's this year's black anyway (maybe . . . )!

**Sagittarians** are always given outdoory, sporty clothes as pressies. Football shirts, anything in their fave teams' colours and big woolly jumpers. But all they really want is a bit of '70s glam. So go to town (steering well clear of Milletts of course) and bring 'em back a glittery acrylic cardi and a pair of crimplene hot pants!

**Capricornians**, notorious for their dislike of extravagance, are always "treated" to cheap 'n' cheerful gifts – shoelaces, a nice egg cup, a manicure set . . . Secretly though, they'd rather have something hideously expensive: in fact, anything that costs less than £1000, as far as they're concerned, is barely worth a thank-you note.

**Aquarians**, outwardly sane but inwardly mad as hatters, are often disappointed to find clothing made of tweed, itchy wool and corduroy in their Christmas stocking. If only people realized how much happier they'd be with some glittery nail polish, false eyelashes and an "I'm With Stupid" T-shirt!

**Pisceans** always get very elegant presents: perfume, original 1940s negligees and silk scarves mainly. But, unbeknown to many, they're actually pretty gauche and would be much happier with a pair of silly sunglasses and a weird wig. (Oh, and don't forget the funny fart cushion!)

**Ariens** are secretly rather glam, but because very few people actually realize this, they're likely to get something very practical for Christmas. They wish their friends and family would stop buying them sensible slippers and handy tool kits, and would splash out on some gorgeously sexy and frivolous undies instead.

## DECEMBER FORECAST

### 1st–7th
Mercury changes signs and surrounds you with secrets. Luckily, you're good at keeping schtum (which is very frustrating for close mates who are desperate for gossip – especially that Gemini friend of yours!) No matter how much you're tempted to blab, keep quiet – you'll get into big trouble otherwise.

**Love:** **Friends:** **Social life:**

### 8th–14th
The Full Moon in your astrological house of money suggests that your spending is getting out of hand. OK, so you want to splash out on pressies for those you love, but you're not Madonna, y'know. Spend within your means or *make* presents if necessary: no one's going to judge you on how much the gifts you give

*See page 176 for key to symbols*

them are worth. (And if they do, you shouldn't be giving them gifts in the first place!)

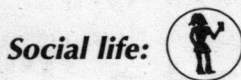

**Love:** (♡)    **Friends:** (☺☺)    **Social life:** (💃)

## 15th—21st
A positive aspect between your ruler Venus and planet of transformation Pluto has you gagging for romance. Choose your new paramour for his personality not his looks and you'll be on the right track. A Xmas party will lead to love – or at the very least an intense, passionate and emotional fling!

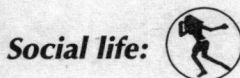

**Love:** (♡♡)    **Friends:** (☺☺)    **Social life:** (🏃)

## 22nd—31st
Energetic Mars enters your opposite sign, causing all sorts of arguments between you and close mates and/or boyfriend/s. It might be an idea to try to reach a compromise before the end of 2000. New Year's Eve could be a painful affair otherwise and it's meant to be fun, so go and enjoy

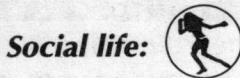

**Love:** (♡♡)    **Friends:** (☺☺)    **Social life:** (🏃)

*See page 176 for key to symbols*

# Part 11:

# Into The New Millennium!

*What does the first part of the new millennium hold for you? How are you and your life going to change in the next decade? To find out the answers to these and a whole load more questions, check out our Ten-Year Forecast . . .*

# Lucky In Love

With Jupiter settled in the money part of your chart luck is indicated, especially on the love front, but only if you think BIG.

The eclipse in January means serious changes with regards to the way you deal with other people. If you're keen to impress a certain someone of the opposite sex this year, do it before mid-March or after mid-August. A retrograde Neptune and Uranus from May till October suggest that you're likely to fall for someone quite unlike anyone you've ever fancied before, but the guy's just not suitable. The eclipse in June forecasts more disruptions in your closest relationships.

Jupiter enters the communications part of your chart from mid-July and helps you get out of a rut. A relative could come into some money, and you could benefit from this. Pluto changing direction in August makes you totally dazzling and able to impress everyone you meet. If you start a new romance you'll be in the driving seat.

Saturn going backwards from the end of September forecasts a sudden lack of cash. From the end of October and throughout November, Uranus is moving forwards and causes you to look for a new direction in life. Remember though – there's a thin line between love and hate and around New Year's Eve you could be discovering just how true that old saying is. You end the year with a passionate romance.

# Life In The Fast Lane

**M**ars warns you that there's much jealousy and resentment around you. Make an effort to avoid people who are masquerading as mates, but who are really nothing of the sort. Saturn changes direction in February and this helps you develop a more responsible attitude towards money. About time . . .

With Pluto following a similar pattern to last year, your love life could be a bit rollercoaster-y between March and August. As energetic Mars changes signs in April, you'll have some excellent money-making ideas. Get things off the ground quickly.

In May, Mars and Venus enter the communications part of your chart and you start to experience life in the fast lane. As Mercury transits three signs in July, you're all over the place, scattering your energy here, there and everywhere. Writing is extremely well-starred between the 7th and 21st, so get scribbling! When Jupiter joins Mars in the home and family part of your chart in August, life at home could be a bit tricky. There may be some upheaval going on – you may even be moving house. Around the same time, money luck is forecast. Unfortunately, a retrograde Saturn in October forecasts money problems; you just can't hang on to it, can you?

There's plenty of love action in November, and December's eclipse coincides with the start of a brand new and passionate relationship. Very nice . . .

# Friends And Lovers 2003

**W**ith lusty Mars in the passion part of your chart, your love life's pretty intense as the New Year dawns. That's not to say it's easy . . . Cooperation and compromise are the answers.

In February, Saturn changes direction; if you've been panicking about money, you can now see light at the end of the tunnel. In March, Uranus changes signs and sees you searching for new friends and/or pastimes. You could be questioning the meaning of love and life during the summer. An eclipse in your opposite sign on 16th May advises you to face up to problems in your most intimate relationship: sort 'em out! Saturn enters the communications part of your chart in June, which could make it difficult for you to get in touch with someone. You'll finally make contact in July. Lucky Jupiter enters the love and fun part of your chart in September and could indicate a romantic interlude. A retrograde Saturn makes October a tense time, connected to that person you were fretting about in June and July. They're up to their old tricks again and this time you've just about had enough! November's eclipse in Taurus may well find you having a clear-out – this could be of your wardrobe, or of your mates.

As Mars changes signs, you realize that someone's got it in for you. Avoid anyone you think might be jealous or envious of you or yours. Keeping a low profile over Christmas and New Year will make you more popular than ever.

# All Change!

Mars remains in the "secrets" part of your chart for the whole of January, making life a bit weird. One so-called mate seems to be doing everything in his/her power to muck things up for you. All you can do is give them a wide berth. If, on the other hand, it's you being the naughty one, now's the time to come clean (or at least stop what you're doing) before it all backfires. By February, you're feeling much more on top of things. At the end of March and for most of April, you should keep a tight rein on your spending.

In May, the eclipse means big changes in your love life and in June, a transiting Mars means the start of even *more* changes – at home this time. The summer, however, will be a joy-filled family-orientated time. Holidays, both at home and away, are well-starred and a holiday romance is a strong possibility. Come September you'll be worn out but happy!

When Mars and Jupiter enter the school/work part of your chart towards the end of September, your ability to plough through work is second to none. You may not be feeling as healthy as you should though, so look after yourself by making sure you're eating, sleeping and exercising enough.

Neptune changes direction in October and this bodes well for your social life. In November, love and fun are well-starred, and just before Christmas, you're lust on legs and can use your sexiness to get whatever (and whoever) you want. Go for it, girl!

# On The Up!

Venus and Mercury changing signs link love to travel. If you're spending the Xmas hols away from home, you could be in for a romantic treat! As Jupiter changes direction in your astrological house of school/work in February, making you take your studies/work more seriously. Saturn has a positive turnaround in March, and this helps you sort out any communication problems.

April's eclipse makes it ultra-important for you to get to know yourself: until you do, you won't know what you really need. The planet of responsibility, Saturn, changes signs in July, causing your love life to be a bit strife-filled. Your relationship has a better chance of success if there's a big age gap between you and your paramour.

Venus enters the work part of your chart in August and this doesn't exactly make it easy for you to get things done. Take some time off if you can. In September, Pluto changes direction and has you feeling passionate! As Jupiter makes its annual transit in October, matters of the heart are looking good. Work goes well too, and someone who previously had it in for you now looks set to become your best mate. In November, expect a few romantic hiccups. In December, Mars imbues you with extra energy, while transiting Venus bodes well for work. Don't underestimate the power of your sex appeal this month – it could get just what you've always wanted.

# Stress And Success

Your ruler Venus changes signs and direction in the first week of January. You're on the brink of major success, but something (or someone) could be holding you back. Make the most of your looks and charisma to get your own way.

In February, Mars in the money part of your chart bodes well for any money-making ideas you might have. A retrograde Mercury and Jupiter in March could cause problems with your social life and love life. Mars moves into the communications part of your chart in April, helping you to make crucial decisions. Mercury, racing through three signs including Taurus for much of May, makes you feel restless. In June, Venus warns you against being over-extravagant. The summer hols get off to a good start, with the emphasis on getting out and about. Your money-making skills are at their peak in August. If you're having trouble with a friend in September, talk things through early in the month.

You're full of energy as October dawns and put most of this into improving your social life: however, there's also a lot of work to be done this month. A transiting Jupiter in November bodes well for friendships. You could be taking on a tad more responsibility at home in December. Christmas will be majorly sexy, with a meeting at a party making the end of the year a truly happy (not to mention memorable) one!

# Heading For The Hills

2007

As 2007 begins, you seem to be putting most of your energies into working out ways of having adventures. Watch out for an Australian or Canadian entering your life around this time. In February, you're likely to be presented with a great opportunity. Take it while you can . . . The eclipse in March causes changes on the romance front: if you continue to be selfish, putting your own needs before everyone else's, you could end up alone. In April, Saturn changes direction and this makes life easier.

In May, Neptune changes direction: any big ideas you have regarding charity work or helping others may have to be put on hold. In June, Mars in Taurus gives you extra energy. Spending time with your family could be fun in early July. Romance is indicated after the 15th. Jupiter starts moving forwards again in August and this boosts your luck. A transiting Saturn in September means a relationship could become trying. Venus makes October a really special time for you. Mars goes backwards in November, meaning that those bright ideas on how you can change your life don't make much sense any more. But don't worry.

Unsolved romantic difficulties rear their ugly heads in December and you could feel like packing your bags and heading for the hills. Might be a good idea to spend Christmas abroad this year.

# A Very Special Year

This year is destined to be a very special one for you. Something happens which is destined to have a profound effect on your life. The meaning of life will preoccupy you for a while. You're looking for answers to almost impossible questions and will be searching in places you've never looked before. Don't become obsessed with this though.

In June, Pluto starts moving backwards, causing you to feel very passionate about someone or something. You could be feeling intensely emotional; do NOT, under any circumstances, dismiss these feelings. The total eclipse in August indicates big changes at home. Many Taureans will be moving away from their family or changing address.

You're feeling hot in September – and that's not down to the weather! You're so sexy that you're totally irresistible. Remember that there is such a thing as too many boyfriends! This could be why October is such a row-filled time for you, especially with regards to your love life. In November, Neptune starts moving forwards and you're easily able to be more generous. You become more attractive and this sees you making new friends. Your mates have got some fab ideas for Christmas, so make sure you listen to them. If you do, Christmas and New Year will be fun-filled and fabulous. Just the way it should be . . .

# Finding Yourself

**W**ith Pluto now settled for the year, you're ready to make some improvements. You could be thinking about using travel or further education to broaden your horizons. Psychic and psychological matters interest you. Many Taureans "find" religion this year.

Throughout February, you'll be concentrating on fulfilling an ambition, but don't neglect everything and everyone else in the process. You've got tons of energy to burn off in March, so now would be a good time to take up a new sport or join a gym. If you're planning to travel between April and September, there could be delays and dilemmas. A new course or job might seem disappointing at the moment, but you'll discover it's just fine later on.

In October, Saturn enters your astrological house of health. If you've not been eating and exercising properly and if you've been burning the candle at both ends, you could come down with nasty lurgies and mystery ailments. Work could be tricky too. By November, you're feeling a lot stronger and more able to stand up for yourself. Your love life's much happier too. As Christmas approaches, you're in a reasonable frame of mind. Your social life improves and certain friends really prove their worth. Your ruler Venus ensures that you're at your most gorgeous over Christmas and New Year and ensures a good time all round. And what more could you want?

# Older And Wiser

As Saturn changes direction, your health could be playing up again: make an effort to take care of yourself. You're thinking about the future when Jupiter changes signs in mid-January. In February, a wise woman will give you some advice. If you're looking for extra cash, now's a good time to ask for it. Mars changes direction in March, giving you the energy and initiative to get out of any trouble you may be in at home.

At the end of May, Uranus enters the social part of your chart and marks the start of a whole new phase of your life. Your attention turns to looking deep within yourself, confronting hidden truths and facing up to stuff you haven't been brave enough to look at before. Jupiter joins Uranus in June, making you extra kind and friendly. Saturn makes a transit in July and helps you concentrate on your career. In August, as Uranus moves backwards for a temporary stay in the social part of your chart, you'll be meeting new mates and losing some old ones. In November, Venus in your opposite sign makes for a pleasant and romantic love life.

You continue to shake off old friends throughout December, but the more you do this, the less painful and more necessary it becomes. Venus puts you in a practical mood over Christmas and New Year. This may make Christmas a bit dull, but all the hard work will be worth it. One thing's for sure: you're not only ten years older than you were at the start of the decade – you're ten years wiser too!

# Part 12:
# Birthday Chart

*Not sure which friend is which star sign? Need an at-a-glance reminder of all your mates' birthdays? Want to know which celeb shares your date of birth? Then fill in this specially devised (starting with Aries and ending with Pisces) birthday chart and fret no more . . .*

## ARIES

### March

**20**

**21** Mark Hamilton (Ash), 1977; Ario (N'Tyce), 1974

**22**

**23** Damon Albarn (Blur), 1968; Marti Pellow, 1966

**24**

**25** Elton John, 1947; Mel (All Saints), 1975

**26**

**27** Mariah Carey, 1969

**28**

**29** Coree (Damage), 1978

**30** Celine Dion, 1968

**31**

### April

**1** Chris Evans and Jean Claude Van Damme, 1966; Phillip Schofield, 1962

**2** Linford Christie, 1960

**3** Will Mellor, 1976

**4** Robert Downey Jnr, 1965

**5**

**6** Chantal (N-Tyce), 1977

**7** Victoria Adams, 1975

8

9

10

11  Cerys Matthews, 1966

12  Paul Nicholls, 1979

13

14

15

16

17

18

19

# TAURUS

20  Luther Vandross, 1951

21  The Queen, 1926

22

23

24  Jas Mann (Babylon Zoo), 1971

25

26

27

28

29  Michelle Pfeiffer, 1958

30

# May

1  Joanna Lumley, 1947

2

**3** Jay Darlington (Kula Shaker), 1969

**4**

**5**

**6**

**7**

**8** Dave Rowntree (Blur), 1964

**9**

**10** Bono (U2), 1960

**11** Harry Enfield, 1961

**12** Emilio Estevez, 1962

**13**

**14** Sinead (B*Witched), 1978; Nat (All Saints), 1973

**15**

**16** Janet Jackson, 1966

**17**

**18**

**19**

**20** Sean Conlon (5ive), 1981; Cher, 1946

# GEMINI

**21**

**22** Naomi Campbell, 1970

**23**

**24**

**25**

**26** Lenny Kravitz, 1964

**27** Paul Gascoigne, 1964; Denise Van Outen, 1974

**28** Kylie Minogue, 1968

**29** Adam Rickitt, 1978; Noel Gallagher, 1967; Mel B, 1975

**30** Sally Whittaker (Coronation Street), 1963

**31**

## June

**1**

**2**

**3**

**4** Noah Wyle, 1971

**5**

**6**

**7** Prince, 1958

**8** Mick Hucknall, 1960

**9** Johnny Depp, 1963; Michael J. Fox, 1961

**10** Liz Hurley, 1965

**11**

**12**

**13** Jason Brown (5ive), 1976

**14** Boy George, 1961

**15** Courtney Cox, 1967

**16**

**17**

**18** Paul McCartney, 1942

**19**

**20** Nicole Kidman, 1966

## CANCER

**21** Prince William, 1982

**22**

**23**

**24**

**25** Jamie Redknapp, 1973; George Michael, 1963

**26**

**27**

**28** Adam Woodyatt (Ian Beale in EastEnders), 1969

**29** Richard Abindin Breen (5ive), 1979

**30**

# July

**1** Keith Duffy (Boyzone), 1974; Pamela Anderson, 1967

**2**

**3** Shane Lynch (Boyzone), 1976; Tom Cruise, 1962

**4**

**5**

**6** Sylvester Stallone, 1946

**7**

**8**

**9** Tom Hanks, 1956

**10** Neil Tennant (Pet Shop Boys), 1954

**11** Richie Sambora (Bon Jovi), 1960

**12** Anna Friel, 1976

**13** Harrison Ford, 1947

**14**

**15**

**16**

**17**

**18**

**19** Anthony Edwards (ER), 1962

**20**

**21** Ross Kemp (EastEnders), 1964; Robin Williams, 1952

**22**

## LEO

23 ------------------------------------

24 ------------------------------------

25 Matt Le Blanc, 1967

26 ------------------------------------

27 ------------------------------------

28 ------------------------------------

29 ------------------------------------

30 Sean Moore (Manic Street Preachers), 1970; Arnold Schwarzenegger, 1947

31 Fatboy Slim, 1963

## August

1 ------------------------------------

2 ------------------------------------

3 ------------------------------------

4 ------------------------------------

5 ------------------------------------

6 Geri Halliwell, 1972; Barbara Windsor (Peggy in EastEnders), 1937

7 David Duchovny, 1960

8 ------------------------------------

9 Whitney Houston, 1963

10 ------------------------------------

11 Andrez (Damage), 1978

12 ------------------------------------

13 ------------------------------------

14 Halle Berry, 1968

15 Mikey Graham, 1972 (Boyzone); Spike (911), 1974

16 Madonna, 1958

17 Robert de Niro, 1943

18 Christian Slater, 1969; Patrick Swayze, 1952

**19**

**20**

**21** Dina Carroll, 1968

**22** Howard Dwayne Dorough (Backstreet Boys), 1973

## VIRGO

**23** Richard Neville (5ive), 1979; Shaun Ryder, 1962

**24** Stephen Fry, 1957

**25** Elvis Costello, 1958

**26** Macaulay Culkin, 1980

**27**

**28**

**29** Michael Jackson, 1958

**30**

**31** Richard Gere, 1949

## September

**1** Gloria Estefan, 1957

**2** Keanu Reeves, 1965

**3** Charlie Sheen, 1965

**4** Kevin Kennedy (Coronation Street), 1961

**5**

**6**

**7**

**8**

**9** Hugh Grant, 1960

**10**

**11**

**12** _____

**13** _____

**14** _____

**15** _____

**16** _____

**17** _____

**18** _____

**19** Jarvis Cocker, 1966; Paul Winterhart (Kula Shaker), 1971

**20** _____

**21** Liam Gallagher, 1972; Jimmy Constable (911), 1973

**22** _____

## LIBRA

**23** _____

**24** _____

**25** Declan Donnelly, 1977; Will Smith, 1968

**26** _____

**27** Lee Anthony Brennan (911), 1975

**28** _____

**29** Brett Anderson (Suede), 1967

**30** _____

## October

**1** _____

**2** Sting, 1952

**3** Kevin Scott Richardson (Backstreet Boys), 1972

**4** Alicia Silverstone, 1976

**5** Kate Winslet, 1975

6

7   Michelle (N-Tyce), 1974

8

9

10

11   Dawn French, 1957

12

13

14   Shaznay (All Saints), 1975; Cliff Richard, 1940

15

16

17

18

19

20   Dannii Minogue, 1970

21   Donna (N-Tyce), 1976

22   Jeff Goldblum, 1952; Zac Hanson, 1985

## SCORPIO

23

24   Alonza Bevan (Kula Shaker), 1970

25

26

27

28   Joaquin Phoenix, 1977; Julia Roberts, 1967

29   Winona Ryder, 1971

30

31

# November

1 ----------------------------------------

2 ----------------------------------------

**3** Ras (Damage), 1976; Roseanne, 1952

**4** Kavanna, 1977; Louise Nurding, 1974

**5** Bryan Adams, 1959

**6** Ethan Hawke, 1970

7 ----------------------------------------

8 ----------------------------------------

9 ----------------------------------------

10 ----------------------------------------

**11** Leonardo DiCaprio, 1974; Demi Moore, 1962

**12** David Schwimmer, 1966

**13** Whoopi Goldberg, 1955

**14** Prince Charles, 1948; Usher, 1978

15 ----------------------------------------

16 ----------------------------------------

**17** Jonathan Ross, 1960; Ike Hanson, 1980

**18** Ant McPartlin , 1975

**19** Meg Ryan, 1961; Jodie Foster, 1962

20 ----------------------------------------

**21** Alex James (Blur), 1968

**22** Scott Robinson (5ive), 1979

# SAGITTARIUS

**23** Zoe Ball, 1970

24 ----------------------------------------

25 ----------------------------------------

**26**   Tina Turner, 1939

**27**

**28**   Dane (Another Level), 1979

**29**   Ryan Giggs, 1973

**30**   Gary Lineker, 1960

# December

**1**

**2**

**3**

**4**

**5**

**6**

**7**   Aaron Carter, 1987; Nic (All Saints), 1974

**8**   Kim Basinger, 1953; Sinead O'Connor, 1966

**9**

**10**

**11**

**12**

**13**

**14**   Michael Owen, 1979

**15**   Adele & Keavey (B*Witched), 1979

**16**

**17**

**18**   Lindsay (B*Witched), 1980; Brad Pitt, 1965; Robson Green, 1964; Stephen Spielberg, 1947

**19**

**20**

**21**   Jamie Theakston, 1970

# CAPRICORN

**22**   Noel Edmonds, 1948

**23**

**24**

**25**

**26**   Jared Leto, 1969

**27**

**28**   Denzel Washington, 1954

**29**

**30**

**31**   Val Kilmer, 1959

## January

**1**   Noel (Damage), 1976

**2**

**3**   Mel Gibson, 1956

**4**   Tim (Ash), 1977; Beth Gibbons (Portishead), 1965; Michael Stipe (REM), 1960

**5**

**6**   Rowan Atkinson, 1956

**7**

**8**   David Bowie, 1947; Karen Poole (Alisha's Attic), 1971

**9**   AJ (Backstreet Boys), 1978

**10**   Rod Stewart, 1945

**11**

**12**   Mel C, 1976

**13**

**14**

**15**

**16**   Kate Moss, 1974

**17** Jim Carrey, 1962

**18** Kevin Costner, 1955; Crispian Mills (Kula Shaker), 1973

**19**

**20** Gary Barlow, 1971

## AQUARIUS

**21** Emma Bunton, 1976

**22**

**23**

**24** Vic Reeves, 1959

**25**

**26**

**27** Mark Owen, 1974

**28** Nick Carter (Backstreet Boys), 1980; Elijah Wood, 1981

**29**

**30**

**31**

## February

**1**

**2**

**3**

**4** Natalie Imbruglia, 1975

**5** Bobby Brown, 1969

**6**

**7** Axl Rose (Guns 'n' Roses), 1962; Danny Goffey (Supergrass), 1974

**8**

**9**

**10**

**11** Brandy (Jennifer Brandy Norwood), 1979

**12** Jade Jones (Damage), 1979

**13** Robbie Williams, 1974

**14**

**15**

**16**

**17**

**18** Matt Dillon, 1964; John Travolta, 1954

## PISCES

**19**

**20** Ian Brown (Stone Roses), 1963; Cindy Crawford, 1966

**21** James Bradfield (Manic Street Preachers), 1969

**22**

**23** Drew Barrymore, 1975

**24**

**25**

**26**

**27** Peter Andre, 1973

**28**

**29**

## March

**1**

**2** Jon Bon Jovi, 1962

**3** Ronan Keating (Boyzone), 1977

**4** Evan Dando, 1967; Patsy Kensit, 1968

**5**

**6** Shaquille O'Neal, 1972

# Birthday Chart

**7**

**8**

**9**

**10** Neneh Cherry, 1964

**11**

**12** Graham Coxon (Blur), 1969; Kelly Bryan (Eternal), 1975

**13** Adam Clayton (U2), 1960

**14** Taylor Hanson, 1983

**15**

**16** Jimmy Nail, 1954

**17** Stephen Gately (Boyzone), 1976

**18**

**19** Bruce Willis, 1955